CAUGHT SHORT ABROAD

WARNING!

REMOVE TROUSERS BEFORE USE

CAUGHT SHORT ABROAD

My U bend romp around the globe

BARTHOLOMEW START

ISBN:1480136700
ISBN-13:9781480136700

For Hannah & Siobhan

Dedicated to Margaret

This book is autobiographical. The events are true, though the names may have changed to save unnecessary embarrassment. Any resemblance to individuals, real or fictional are purely coincidental.

This book is dedicated to anyone who has been 'caught short'. I trust you can feel a certain empathy with my plight.

Being in need of an evacuation in Milton Keynes can be just as harrowing as wanting one in Marrakesh. Though, it is far more likely in the latter!

Continue to poo as long as you live, it is something you will never tire of, and it will give you hours of pleasure.

Reliving your 'stool' tales down the pub can make for a memorable night.

Ironically at which point, you will probably be sitting on a stool.

Happy crapping!

This book was written as a collection of totally unrelated short stories, based on the authors issues in the toilet over the last 30 years. It was not the authors intention to write a novel or a travel book. The stories are not meant to offend the reader in any way.

The style of writing is deliberate, although if you are upset by the grammar and the style, you should have been an English teacher. The author wanted to maintain the rawness of the subject matter.

Please read it in the manner it is intended, with a smile on your face.

Everyone goes to the toilet, it is a fact of life. Everyone has been caught short at some point, and whilst it may not have been amusing at the time, I am sure you have seen the funny side since.

If you do not like toilet humour – read no further.

However, If you do – Forget your troubles for a few hours and have a good laugh.

Bartholomew Start

CRAPOMETER

Ghost poo – The perfect poo – no effort, no waste, no flush, no wipe.

Killer poo – The poo with corners on it – who said you can't fit a square peg in a round hole.

Stripe poo – usually a two day old poo which starts one colour and ends up being a few shades lighter or darker.

Sultana poo – A most disappointing effort – spend half an hour pushing and the result is a sheep size dropping in the pan.

The Elvis killer – pokes out the top of the water line and has trouble being flushed. Usually happens when visiting someone's home.

The hot tar poo – sticks like shit to a blanket – after 50 wipes there is still more.

The second thought poo – Just when you thought you'd finished – trousers up, then immediately back down.

The fisherman poo – No matter how many times you flush. It keeps bobbing to the surface. Usually need toilet paper to weigh it down.

"*Pleased to meet Poo*"

Meeting the 'in-laws' for the very first time can be a harrowing experience, especially when you don't speak the 'lingo'.

My girlfriend was Polish, in the days before the Polish Armada arrived on our shores. At the time, people joked I had got her in a magazine for lonely hearts. How the hell did they find out?

In 1990, an Englishman arriving in a small town in Central Poland was a bit of a novelty. Indeed, only a year earlier an exchange student from Tanzania, had caused mayhem when he appeared in the town square, as literally hundreds of locals hung out of their windows, to 'gawp' at the dark stranger from warmer climes. My arrival behind the Iron Curtain' was a little less newsworthy.

The town of Blonie is just outside Warsaw and has the rather dubious reputation - in a country known for its excessive drinking, of being the alcohol capital of Poland.

Napoleon had stayed the night in Blonie *en route* to conquering Prussia, and had remarked,

"This is a dull little town in the middle of nowhere".

I expect his famous phrase: "Not tonight Josephine" referred to his not wanting to stay more than a single night in Blonie.

There were drunkards everywhere, queuing for food, serving in shops, driving buses and serving communion at mass. Absolutely everyone was inebriated. It was actually quite difficult to find anyone who wasn't under the influence of drink. Even dogs in the street were half cut.

There were hordes of bison breathed locals swigging neat alcohol out of brown paper bags, hanging around street corners, shouting obscenities at passing old ladies, and generally knocking seven bells out of each other - and that was the local police force. It made me smile, as I thought perhaps all the propaganda about life behind the Iron Curtain might just be true.

Hindsight is all well and good, and yes with hindsight, I should have gone to the toilet in Denmark or at least on the plane.

It had been a long time since the flight left Copenhagen and I knew I needed the toilet just after we left Warsaw International airport, but you always think I'll wait.

Four hours later, as I walked up the path of the family home in the Polish countryside, I was virtually 'touching cloth'.

I raced into the house and formally, if a little speedily, introduced myself to the waiting crowd. After a few minutes of nodding and hand shaking, I found myself alone in a bathroom, that had seen better days. Now I must warn you that the plumbing system in Poland at the time, left a lot to be desired, and the toilet flush, was not the most powerful.

After I had finished my ablutions, I returned to the kitchen, where my girlfriend made me a cup of tea, told me to relax and she went out of the room.

A few minutes passed, when suddenly I heard a commotion near the bathroom. I got up and went to see what all the shouting was about, after all, Polish people having a serious discussion - when you don't understand a word - always seems more dramatic.

To my horror there were four people in the bathroom, all looking down the toilet, having what appeared to be a heated debate - her auntie had a broom handle and was forcing it down the toilet and babbling in forked tongues.

Her mother, who minutes earlier hadn't known me from Adam, sounded quite cross, so I asked my girlfriend what everyone was saying.

She told me, that her mum was - perturbed by an enormous turd that had blocked the toilet, and 'someone' had put down too much toilet paper.

At this point they all turned and looked at me. I put my head down in shame, as her auntie forced the broom handle down the toilet again, forcing all the water to turn brown, and cursed in Polish:

"What a stubborn turd!"

Her father was far more pragmatic, and whilst he pulled a face, that suggested he wasn't totally at ease, standing in the stench filled room, or that his daughter was seeing a bloke who smelled like a slurry truck, patted me on the back and said – "These things happen."

The Lord works in mysterious Poos

While working my way round the world, I stayed for several months picking various fruit on the Greek mainland.

During a particularly lean period, I was forced into the mountains of the Northern Peloponese to pick grapes, like an elephant searching for water in Etosha National park, having to travel hundreds of miles to make ends meet.

The village we stayed in was tiny and had very limited accommodation, so during the grape picking season the village priest was asked to put workers up at the local monastery.

Migrant workers slept in the aisle of the monastery in sleeping bags.

After putting in a particularly impressive shift, a beaming Greek farmer asked me to come for supper at his '*speti*'. His wife had made a rather tasty potato and steak meal, which had been soaked in an alarmingly excessive amount of olive oil. Though scrumptious, I knew the amount of olive oil I was digesting would cause trouble. Could I afford the laundry bill?

It was a brief thought that would come back to haunt me several hours later, and render me out the game for two or three days.

As I settled into my sleeping bag for the night, the pain started, and as the hours passed, the pain got more intense, and shifted lower down. I waited as long as I could, until I couldn't hold it in anymore. The last shooting pain dropped the bulk of the olive oil soaked steak into 'the loading bay'. I struggled with the zip of my sleeping bag in a desperate attempt to get out of it. As I hurtled down the aisle, buttocks clenched, and sweating profusely, I knew I wouldn't make it. I managed to get to the door but no further. Squatting down, I desecrated the steps of this holy place with a mixture of relief and shame.

I was squatting on the steps for ages, so much so, if a local had passed, they'd have thought I was a newly carved statue, a sentinel guarding the gates of heaven. It was never ending, like watching a five - day test match between two not particularly talented sides. When I had finished, the steps were in a terrible state, as was my sphincter - swollen like a blood orange. I realized, with some concern, that I didn't have any toilet paper.

How embarrassing to be left like a puppy sitting next to its own mess. I was dressed in my shorts and only had my money belt. Deciding not to rip some pages out of my passport was one of the best decisions I've ever made. Opting for the only possible solution to my dilemma, I took my shorts off and used them - as best I could - to clean myself up.

I didn't know what to do with my badly soiled shorts; I certainly couldn't put them back on, that would be social suicide, a fashion *'faux pas'*. Then like the blinding light that knocked St Paul off his horse, on the road to Damascus, it came to me, I would throw them on the monastery roof. I couldn't possibly throw them as far as the main monastery roof. However, there was a porch area at the front, which could be the final resting place for my now defunct shorts.

I threw them up as far as I could, and they landed out of sight on the sloping vestibule.

Due to the trauma and sickness, I was totally drained and went back into the monastery to sleep before starting work. Exhausted and too weak from the previous night's ordeal, I was unable to wake at six o clock to leave for work with the other grape pickers.

I failed to warn them of the catastrophic sight that they would be greeted with upon opening the main door. To my horror a Scottish lad was first out in the watery autumnal sunshine. He was aghast at the carnage left on the steps, and shouted, "Christ, - a donkey has been in the night and shat on the steps. Good god, you'd think the farmer would tether it." I didn't have the nerve to mention I'd done it.

Some days later, I had recovered sufficiently to go back to work - I was walking back with the others to the monastery, when we noticed the priest up on the roof. He never said anything about my shorts, but a day later we were all asked to leave the village under a cloud. To this day the others are puzzled by the way the whole village suddenly turned against us. My lips are sealed of course, unlike my bottom on that occasion.

The language of LVOV

The food in Ukraine is rather odd for a Western European palate: pork fat covered with chocolate is just one example.

On arrival in Lvov after a very long train journey from Warszawa, I was absolutely starving and needing sustenance. Not knowing where to eat, I stumbled upon a small café style eatery, which served what looked like traditional Ukrainian fare. That was the problem, Ukrainian fare. Salted pork fat dipped in chocolate may be like an elephant seal to a Great White in these parts, but to a Western palate, it spelt a serious trip to the toilet at best, and a change of underwear.

Now I admit, I did have a few beers the night before, just to help me sleep you understand,– well it was a main road, and I had terrible trouble trying to fully close the window. The traffic noise from the street below was like the shelling of a Beirut suburb. One of the hinges had come off and the rest of the window was held in place with little more than fishing wire and chewing gum.

I woke the next morning with a slight hangover. The sunlight was blindingly bright, due to the threadbare nature of the cheap, but not remotely cheerful curtains.

Completely naked, I got out of bed and went to the window, to have a look at Lvov in daylight. The evening before, it had resembled a Wild West frontier town, and I was keen to see it in all its glory. Lvov on the other hand, was not ready to see me in all my glory.

The old net curtains covered my embarrassment, but as I peered out, a sudden urge to pass wind came over me. What followed was particularly upsetting, and I was relieved the net curtains had seen better days.

I don't often do it, indeed, I pride myself on never having stains in my underpants, but on this occasion, as I farted, I actually followed through. Technically, a totally different animal, the medical term for it is 'shart'. The 'shart' is a common complaint amongst children under the age of four, and 'wino's' over thirty.

The problem was, it squirted onto the net curtains. I was appalled, as I'd never soiled myself in such a way before.

It was not a particularly bad stain, but it smelled to high heaven. How would I feel, or should I say, how would the cleaner feel, when she entered the room and was confronted with such a ripe smelling gravy stain.

There was only one thing for it - apart from setting fire to the net curtains, which may land me in jail or hospital, or jumping to my impending death, equally unacceptable ends to my, as yet unfulfilled life - I would have to mask the smell with a cunning plan.

I made myself a coffee to ponder my options, - Then I had a light bulb eureka moment whilst holding my cup. That was it: the coffee. I used the last remnants of coffee from the sachet to rub over the offending stain. Pleased with my handy work, I bent down and quickly sniffed the new coffee stain for authenticity. Whilst not the comfortable and welcoming aroma of a newly opened jar of Nescafe - I think I got away with it!

I resorted to eating McDonald's for the remainder of my trip.

Drop your guts

In the spring of 1986, after a considerable length of time spent working 77 hours a week in the mountains of Nepal - for the princely sum of $US2 per week, that's right $US2 a week, not an hour - I had my fill of being a waiter. After three months living solely of curried lentils and rice three times a day, I feared that if my western palate was subjected to anymore of this bland diet, it may well kill me off, or have a long term affect on my health.

Under my arms smelt of curried lentils, nothing could mask it: spraying myself head to toe in that very masculine fragrance *Hi Karate* made it worse.

I'd already had cholera and ghardia, but I'll leave the cholera for another story. Suffice to say the affects of ghardia: an amoebic disorder that covers your stools in a mucus membrane, and renders your bowels uncontrollable for weeks on end, with the socially unacceptable after affects of senseless farting, that smelled so obnoxious, when you let rip, you could literally cut the air with a knife.

The M6 was once closed for several hours, due to a lorry driver returning from a trip to India with a bout of ghardia. They said it was fog, but I knew the real reason. Why do you think airports close quite often during foggy days, it's not the weather, its passengers returning from India with a bowel disorder.

After flying in from Bombay, my ghardia was so severe, that when I broke wind in Northampton - upon my return to England - I managed, with a mixed sense of shame and pride in equal measure, to clear a 24 table snooker hall, quicker than an escaped tiger at Chester zoo. People ran for their lives.

The room was still empty twenty minutes after I'd the misfortune to 'drop my guts'. Indeed, the snooker hall manager, - was quite annoyed about it, asked for my membership card, and in a fit of rage, tore it up in front of me, saying I was to be given a life time ban.

A national first - barred for impersonating a skunk.

Suffering a second bout of uncontrollable flatulence, I passed wind in the lobby on my way out - just for good measure. That'll teach him I thought. The doorman said with menace

"Drop your guts again mate and I'll drop you!! Like a skunk, I scurried away.

The air hung heavy, like the smog over Athens, when you leave the port of Piraeus. The smell clung to every fibre of my ill-fitting trousers; after all I had lost nearly two stone in weight. I was beginning to become a social misfit. Everywhere I went I would break wind, and trade around the pubs of Northampton started to suffer as a result.

Even my friends stopped asking me out for a pint, they said my farts curdled the beer and that their partners could smell flatulence on their clothes when they got home, just like cigarette smoke used to linger after a night in the pub.

One couple actually broke up over my smell. He found it amusing, but she found it disgusting, they started arguing about being childish, the next thing she puts two fingers up to him and walked off shouting: "you were rubbish in bed anyway!!"

It was my mum who finally put an end to the humiliation. She said: "Go to the doctor's - you can't carry on like this".

I think she actually meant - go see a vet.

Seeking medical advice, the doctor who actually mouthed the words "Phew - Good Lord!!!" on asking me to reproduce the fetid smell for him to diagnose - which to be honest didn't take long, as the flatulence was - like the winds up in Shetland - wild and unrelenting, put me, rather swiftly, on a course of Flagyl tablets, and showed me the door.

He asked his secretary to hold all appointments for fifteen minutes whilst he opened the window and left the room himself.

These tablets were fantastic, extremely potent and cleared up the amoebic disorder in a number of weeks, but rendered my bowel inoperable for several days.

The boast of the bottle was that - they could dry up Lake Winnipeg. After taking them, I would not doubt it!

Land of the midnight flatulence

On a recent trip to Iceland I happened to be flicking through the TV channels, after all, 23 hours of daylight means you have time on your hands, and there is only so much puffin you can eat, or whales you can watch.

As Mr Mannering commented in an episode of *Dad's Army*, in which the platoon were impressed that he could play the bag pipes, when asked where he'd learned, he replied dryly "On my honeymoon in Scotland – the days were long but the nights were even longer."

I was only mildly interested in the Russian Eurovision entry, of four Russian women of indeterminable age. My interest waned however, when the Serbian entry began to warble like a song thrush in his mother tongue.

I turned to channel seven, which was showing a Rick Moranis hit comedy, in English - with Icelandic sub titles, which I realised after a few dull minutes, would have been funnier if it had been in Icelandic with no sub titles. The fact it starred Rick Moranis neither qualified it as a hit or a comedy.

By far the most entertaining channel was an episode, in English of *Embarrassing Bodies*. The whole half hour was devoted to flatulence. It caught my interest immediately. Apparently they surveyed ten thousand people, and remarkably three percent said they had never farted in their lives, presumably these three percent had been women, and probably religious.

According to the survey - People pass wind somewhere between ten and fifteen times a day. However, the most alarming statistic, which made me put down my Great Auk sandwich, was that anyone dropping their guts more than twenty five times a day, had bowel issues and should seek an immediate consultation with a doctor.

 I noted with curiosity that there was no statistic for people who' let one go' – twenty times an hour. Presumably, if they had bothered to quote those formidable stats, the advice given would be, "Run for the hills."

So armed with my newly acquired data, I

decided to do a survey on myself, and I would count how many times I passed wind. After two days I was slightly deflated and ashamed, literally, to count a dismal tally, of trumping only eighteen times on both days. Obviously that did not include any seepage during sleep.

Like evaporation from the Persian Gulf, the loss is incalculable.

The criteria for what passed as a 'trump' had me howling. Tears streamed down my face, as they explained that two or three trumps in quick succession, like an escaped convict playing percussion in an orchestra - only counted as 'one wind movement.'

It also went on to describe how 'pigeons escaping from a cardboard box' just prior to an evacuation – did not count at all.

Nevertheless, just eighteen, was a dismal return. I decided - like my school report had said at the end of most terms: "I must try harder" - I would try again, but this time, I would eat a whole bag of dried apricots.

I'm normally quite 'windy' after just a handful, but after a whole packet, it was a remarkable transformation, from Beaufort scale three –

gentle breeze to force twelve – a hurricane.

My lower bowel ran like a racing car after a prolonged pit stop. Smooth as honey on a hot rock.

Just four hours into my 'fartathon' I had passed the benchmark of twenty-five. At the end of the day, like a Buddhist prayer flag flapping on the slopes of Everest base camp, my sphincter was in tatters.

Clocking up a mind boggling fifty-nine, almost as much as a vegan can produce, on a diet of mung bean salad and soya milk.

I was certainly up there with farmyard livestock as a major contributor to the melting of the Polar ice caps. But, at that moment CO_2 emissions and political correctness, were the last things on my mind.

 I was content, as relaxed in spirit as my sphincter was.

 As I climbed in to bed at the end of such a momentous day, I squeezed out number sixty, lay on my pillow, and smiled with pride – reaching for the tube of *Anusol.*

The sunlight still glared through the window, although the hour was late, nearly 11:30 at night, thank god for the long hours, in the land of the midnight flatulence.

"Where's my trousers?"

After a particularly heavy night on the beer in Alexandropolis, it was with clenched cheek that we boarded the train bound for Istanbul. The last ouzo chaser the night before - whilst arm wrestling a local welder for one last beer had seemed a good idea at the time, but now seemed nothing short of greedy.

 Although the sun was shining and I was looking forward to arriving in Istanbul - a place I'd wanted to visit since watching *'Midnight Express'* the rumblings in my stomach - were not a good omen!

My companion had been drinking slightly more ouzo than me, he looked rather uncomfortable, but in a reflective mood, as he lifted his heavy rucksack on to his shoulder. Relieved that the strain had been safely dealt with, we boarded the train and started to look for a spare carriage with two empty seats. It was July and crowded with holidaymakers, although not many Greeks. As we know the Greeks refuse to acknowledge that Turkey exists.

We passed several carriages until we found a suitable resting place, with two empty seats.

Miguel lifted his own rucksack onto the luggage racks above our heads, with little difficulty. After all, he was 6ft 2inches. I asked him if he could put mine up on the rack with his. Unfortunately, unprepared for the additional weight of our camping equipment, he shocked the six other people in the carriage – including a pregnant lady and small impressionable child, as he farted under the strain.

There was a deathly silence, and then a look from Miguel that will haunt me to my dying day.

He bit his lip and rolled his eyes, as he had evidently 'sharted'. Wearing no underpants the stain expanded into the fabric of his khaki trousers, like a plague of locusts devouring a field of corn.

He backed out of the carriage and slithered away to the nearest toilet.

Some considerable time later, I caught a glimpse of him frantically trying to attract my attention. At this point I noticed he wasn't wearing any pants and was desperately trying to cover his 'tackle' with a T-shirt, two sizes too small.

I ran out of the carriage to ask him what was going on. He started his sorry tale and began to laugh. In the toilet washing his trousers, he realized that they would take ages to dry, and hit on a brain wave:

He noticed that the toilet window was open, and thought if he held them out of the window - with the warm summer air and a speeding train, they would be dry in no time at all.

As he held on to his Sunday best, he did not contemplate that a train doing equally high speed may be going in the opposite direction.

The force of the two passing trains causing a swirling mass of air, pulled the waistband from his grip, and launching his trousers into the Greek undergrowth, never to be seen again.

He asked if I could lend him a pair of shorts until we arrived in Istanbul. How could I refuse?

Indeed me being 5 ft 7 and Miguel being 6 ft 2 meant he would certainly launch the myth in

Istanbul at least - that all Englishmen were hung like 'Grand National winners', as he stepped off the train wearing bright red shorts that were five sizes too small.

"And how would you like that wrapped Sir?"

When I left school I went to work for a rather exclusive kitchen and bathroom showroom in Northampton, as a trainee designer.

The company was very proud of its rich clientele and the salesmen boasted - in the privacy of the office - at the size of the sales they generated individually, and as a whole.

One Saturday, a bathroom salesman showed a young couple with a child around the showroom. At one point the child was left to wander on his own, whilst the salesman bestowed the virtues of gold finished, half-flush option on a Royal Doulton suite.

It is obvious now, what actually happened and where the young boy had disappeared.

Later that day, the bathroom manager had a very important client coming in from Bedfordshire, to choose a new bathroom for his newly converted barn.

He didn't usually show people around, but on this occasion decided he would be heavily involved in the sale.

As he got to the most expensive bathroom range in the showroom, he turned to the Arab, and with a great deal of pride stated: "And of course this sir is our Jacob Delefon suite, the top of the range." Smiling, he lifted the toilet seat and said: "Just look at the quality of that."

To his horror he peered into the toilet to find a great steaming welt of a turd staring up at them both. The Arab frowned and asked: "Is that included in the price?"

The child had obviously thought the display was a real bathroom, with a fully functioning plumbing system, and had decided to use the toilet as it had been intended.

Needless to say he did not get the sale, and to make matters worse, his senior manager made him remove the offending turd with a pair of *Marigolds*, and clean around the bowl with Jiff and a toothbrush.

From that day on the term 'Dirty Arab' had a completely new meaning in the bathroom department.

Sadly, his career never recovered. He was demoted to assistant manager and never showed another high profile client around again. He started to hit the bottle and appeared at work unkempt and unshaven.

The last we heard he had gone feral and was last seen drinking cans of Tenants Super and selling the Big Issue!!

"And all because the little boy loved Milk Tray"

A Good Jobbie

Some time ago I decided I needed a change of scenery regarding my career. So I joined an agency to see what might turn up.

After several telephone interviews I found myself in the reception of a famous multinational bank in Cheshire - waiting to be interviewed for a job in IT. As suspected, the pre interview nerves, coupled with two strong cups of coffee, and the fact that on that particular morning , in my haste to avoid rush hour traffic, I hadn't actually 'gone', which culminated in me wanting to 'go'.

Sitting at the reception desk were two extremely attractive pneumatic twenty something's. I was desperate to go to the toilet, and worried about my impending interview.

I made a subconscious note that the GENTS were immediately to the left of the reception desk.

I had twenty minutes to wait until my interview and thought that would be sufficient time to 'go'. So, taking the bull by the horns, I 'went', quicker than I thought, although at the time I noted, it was a little bit 'whiffy' to say the least.

The girls on reception knew where I was, and why, but it was slightly embarrassing to think I would have to go back out and sit opposite them. I would have settled for that, in the same way England would settle, for a draw against Spain in a football tournament, before the kick off.

And - kick off it most definitely did!!! In the main reception, soon after I'd locked the door and dropped my trousers around my ankles.

I finished performing, and mercifully noticed that the toilet had an extractor fan. I pulled the string of what I thought was the extractor fan, but to my abject horror, trousers around my ankles, I'd pulled the chord of the emergency alarm.

The noise was deafening, and to make matters worse - made no difference to the 'whiff' in the room. A crowd gathered by the door thinking I was in some need of medical assistance. Now everyone in the building had been alerted to my homemade 'emanation'.

The only assistance I required now was a ladder, to climb out of the window - run across the car park, and get back into my car, and drive as fast as I could, back to Liverpool. Failing that, I could follow my turd into the toilet and escape, like Tim Robbins in The Shawshank Redemption.

A sense of resignation to the imminent embarrassing low I would face crept over me, as I speedily pulled my pants up, I heard the two girls on reception saying: "Is anyone in there. Are you alright?"

Unfortunately I wasn't, far from it. I wanted to end my life right there, if I had a gun, I would have shot myself – twice for good measure.

I heard a voice from within say meekly: "Yes I'm ok."

The next sentence was the one I'd feared most: "Let us in, we need to disable the alarm."

Let them in I thought, I wouldn't let my worst enemy in at that moment, to this ungodly bouquet. It was at that point that my legs actually buckled from under me.

I slumped down on the toilet, leaned forward, and with an extremely heavy heart, and empty bowel, opened the door.

The look of disgust on their two faces as they entered the 'throne' room was one of utter revulsion, as the smell hit them, head on, like a punch from Mike Tyson.

One of the girls looked me right in the eye and shook her head. I lowered my eyes and shook mine too, but for a completely different reason.

The braver of the two girls gave an audible "phew" and started to fiddle above my head with the alarm.

Thank the Lord - the alarm stopped. They both then looked at each other, as Mike Tyson gave another hammer blow, but this time the punch in the face was aimed in my direction. They both sniggered and went back to the reception desk. I trundled out like a sad abused cat, to a room full of extremely stern faces. I sat down bowed my head, and like a criminal at the gallows, awaited my sentence.

I looked up occasionally to see the two girls looking in my general direction. They appeared to frown in a belittling manner. The sniggering continued, and that look – like I was something they had stepped in – to be honest the toilet did smell like something they had stepped in, and probably would until mid morning.

I wanted the ground to open up before me, and take me to a less painful place.

Burning in hell would have hurt less.

I never found out if it was my lack of IT expertise, or the fact I had thrown in the towel before the interview started, but I never got the job, and thankfully I don't bank there either.

I am happy to give it a wide berth, so our paths will never cross, unlike the two chords in the toilet.

Since then – No matter how smelly the aftermath of a bowel movement - If I have to go in a public toilet, I don't under any circumstances activate the extractor fan.

If someone is waiting outside, then it is far less embarrassing to own up – hands aloft - and say to them: "I'd wait 5 minutes if I were you mate".

Jobbie Done!

Chinese Poo??

Polish people are quite odd. I should know - I married one. My wife went through many health fads, and at a drunken New Year's Eve party, I was waiting for the bathroom, and accidentally walked in on her. I was greeted to the sight of her drinking her own urine. Believe it or not, drinking your own 'aqua vita' is beneficial to the immune system.

The only thing it made me immune to, was kissing her at the stroke of midnight. I had noticed a slight nasty aroma earlier in the night, when I had been talking to her, but I put it down to the snaps we were drinking. The smell was particularly unpleasant. Not dissimilar to walking down a back alley and finding a disused tramps sleeping bag. She asked me why I pulled a face! She thought I was the odd one. I ask you!!

I never tried it myself, but my wife and her mother swore by it. I in turn, swore at them for doing it. But I would say that wouldn't I.

Allegedly! - the first of the day is particularly

rich in minerals and nutrients, when the urine is so yellow it is almost brown.

In olive oil terms, that would be the 'cold pressed' or 'first pressing'.

It was on one morning after a quick kiss I commented on her fetid breath, and told her to do something about it, or a divorce was imminent. As it happens, unbeknown to me at the time, a divorce was imminent, but due to her running off with an Italian colleague from IBM, not due to the diabolical fumes steaming off her. Perhaps that was how she lured him! The gargling -'wee wee' siren.

Anyway - I haven't eaten *Spaghetti Bolognaise* since!

We got into a quite heated debate, about the virtues of drinking 'your own piss', and she told me that lots of celebrities drink their own home brew.

I asked her to name one; the only one she could come up with was Sarah Miles. Hardly a celebrity these days, and regardless of her celebrity status, she is well known in Hollywood as 'barking mad'. I retorted, rather sarcastically: "Sarah Miles - Oh well, that's alright then. Let's all start drinking our own piss, you lunatic."

Anyway, as she was eulogizing about the famous people who bestow the virtues of carrying out such a socially unacceptable act, She said, "...And you know, the Chinese Prime Minister..."

She paused at this point, and I replied after a few seconds, "Eats Poo?" She replied: "Oh - I don't actually know his name!"

As you can imagine I roared with laughter.

The Goan Pigs

Whilst travelling on an extremely tight budget in Goa, and by tight I mean $5 a day, I needed somewhere to rest my weary head.

As you can imagine my choice of accommodation was a little limited. I had thought about sleeping on Colva beach, a picture perfect vista by day, but at night, rabid dogs patrolled the shoreline and incessant barking, would have kept Rip Van Winkle awake.

The best chance of me getting a good eight hours sleep - was to ask a local fisherman if I could hire a room in his house. Mr Rodriquez was a very jolly, plump chap. He was extremely dark. Wearing little more than a handkerchief for a loincloth, it hardly covered a postage stamp, never mind his privates, which, from where I was standing, were extremely public. He had nothing to cover his embarrassment, so there was no chance of him covering his enormous 'behind'.

At one point he bent down, and the ambient temperature of the whole region dropped by two degrees, as his enormous rump cast Western India into shade. However, there was one big plus about Mr Rodriquez: He wanted to improve his English and didn't appear to understand the concept of money.

There are tribes in the Amazon with more fiscal acumen than Mr Rodriquez. So, for the princely sum of $2 a day, I had a beach front room in one of the world's most splendid paradises. What is more, he had moved himself and his wife out, to sleep on the veranda, whilst I slept in his bed. His bedroom was a generic term, as the furniture had seen better days. Indeed, the room was so untidy, and it looked like it had taken the brunt of a recent cyclone. Still, I was safe in the knowledge that if a tsunami hit in the night, nothing would get passed that fat arse of his.

He also insisted in letting me eat with the family, for free. This bloke would have given Conrad Hilton a run for his money - as entrepreneur of the year.

Though free, the food was a little bland. Fish, followed by fish, washed down with more fish! They did have some rice and fruit and vegetables came in the guise of star fruit off the tree with an occasional coconut and mango.

I dropped the occasional mango and coconut myself. It was difficult not to in India. Everyone ends up with 'the runs'. It is inevitable as paying taxes and dying.

No one escapes, not even the Indians. We call it 'Bombay belly', The Indians call it 'Accrington arse'.

The cost was a huge plus to staying with the Rodriquez family.

There was a down side – no toilet. In a land where you are more likely to get the 'squitters', than a suntan, it was a dilemma.

It is hard to believe that in Goa, where the sun shines constantly for six months, at an equitable 32C - it would be more difficult to not get a tan, but I suppose spending so much time in the *karsie* limited the opportunity to sunbathe.

Tourist - come back from India, looking like they have spent the last six years in solitary confinement, in a prisoner of war camp.

I asked him where the toilet was, but his Portuguese/English was absolutely awful, and he resorted to a bizarre mime, which was like watching a rude game of charades after the 9 pm watershed. He kept squatting down only for his left testicle to pop out. He would smile, reach in to his ill-fitting loincloth and put it back.

The top and bottom of it – an apt phrase, was that, basically when they needed to go, they crapped in the forest.

He walked me about 100m from the house to a small mound, behind which were lots of smaller mounds of the human kind. On top of this mound of earth - covered with flies and biting ants - was a broken drainpipe precariously perched, and slanting downward towards a rancid pit of poo?

For privacy, his longsuffering wife had woven a panel out of banana leaves. It was stuck in the ground, shielding the view from the house, but on the three other sides, you were basically performing feral. Open to the elements.

To make matters worse there was no toilet paper.

Instead, there was an old tin full of brown water, with which the incumbent squatter-

cleaned themselves-using their left hand. In ancient Rome, they were more civilized!

Earlier in the day I caused quite a stir, by dipping into the communal rice bowl at lunchtime with my left hand. A culinary 'no no'

Upon my first trip to the toilet, I could not believe what happened. I wandered into the forest in the general direction of the banana panel. Suddenly a group of wild pigs came running from the trees. I nearly filled my pants in fright. They ran past me making excited pig noises and gathered round the earth mound at the bottom of the ordure filled cesspit.

They jockeyed for position, as I gingerly perched my bare behind on the drainpipe.

At this point, the thought of people watching me was far from my mind. I was more worried about the pigs, and possibly falling backward into my own feculence.

As I forced one out with ease - too much breadfruit and mango - I suspected - I heard squabbling behind me. The pigs were actually fighting over my shite. The biggest pig won the battle. As I looked down in horror, he looked up at me, with a hint of admiration.

He had a little bit of poo on the end of his nose, and, as I looked away, the sun light caught his eye, and he appeared to wink at me, as if to say: "Thanks a lot".

Buses always come in Number Two's

By far the most uncomfortable feeling anyone can possibly have, apart from - accidentally meeting your lover with her husband at the checkout - is being desperate to take a dump and having to 'hang on'. Forget bursting for a piss - for some reason, whilst that is certainly uncomfortable, and if you wait long enough quite painful - it doesn't come close.

But, and like Clarissa Dixon Wright, it's a big butt, the rewards when you finally unload are almost orgasmic. The agony and the ecstasy I call it. Nothing brings on a blind panic more than hanging on to a 'turtle head' when you know you are along way from the nearest toilet, well, perhaps losing your passport at check in, but not much else.

If you asked Stephen Hawking what ten multiplied by ten is if he needed to take a dump, he would be incapable of telling you - his mind as empty as a goldfish.

Forget black holes, the only hole he'd be interested in at that particular moment would be his arse hole.

For some reason, the urgent need to empty ones bowels, can manifest into primeval uncontrollable twitching, and squirming that happen under no other circumstance. Rather like a temporary bout of Tourettes- Syndrome.

For a start, you physically start to sweat. Absolutely everywhere! It can be minus 27C in the Yukon; Polar bears can be fighting on an ice flow, but the prospect of 'soiling yourself', brings you out in a heat rash.

Once it is in the 'loading bay' and the bomb doors have been activated, not even running to the toilet helps. Indeed, by an awful quirk of nature, rushing to the toilet is the worst thing you can do. It is human nature, at 'target locked' stage - the point of no return - to actually walk in slow motion to avoid a premature trip to the laundrette.

On one such occasion, in Calcutta; where everyone barring locals, are in a perpetual state of 'Bomb bay' red alert: Like a caterpillar looking for leaves, the foreigner is always, on a constant vigil to find 'the bog'.

I was on a bus heading down the main thoroughfare - Chowringhee Street; I was just passing the Calcutta Museum near Sudder Street, so I knew it was ages until my hostel stop.

Suddenly, the shooting pains started, I knew rice water wasn't far behind, I needed to evacuate, and NOW.

I didn't really care where I was in a city of nine million – nor, that it would be a long wait for another bus - all I cared about, was getting rid of last night's supper. I didn't care where, anywhere, except the shorts I was wearing.

The bell rang for the bus to stop, it may have only been one dull note, but it was music to my ears. Remember the TV series *Name That Tune* - "Well Tom, I'll name it in one." And as quickly as my tightly clenched buttocks would allow, I made my way to the front door.

I was so alarmed by my predicament that I didn't even wait for the bus to come to a complete standstill - it was still moving, and so was my arse. I jumped off, completely oblivious to the crowd gathered at the bus stop.

I let out a joyous "Ahhh" as I'd managed not to

fill my freshly laundered shorts.

Sadly my joy was short lived as my own "Ah Bisto" moment stopped several commuters in the tracks. The throng of people waiting to get on the already crowded bus were less than understanding.

Unconcerned that I'd just done my business in front of them, yet agitated that I might make them late for work!

I was still in a squatting position, when I looked up and caught the eye of a waiting nun, who was just in the process of straddling me to get on the bus.

I nodded and smiled from the filthy street - and said "Morning", she nodded knowingly, as if she too had once been caught out in the cat and mouse game of under garment 'Russian roulette'.

I had now joined the under-class, the untouchables. She knew it and I new it. Had no one got an ounce of shame left - I thought?

In all my confusion and haste, I realized - I had left my rucksack on the bus. My misery was complete. An arm appeared from the window, holding my rucksack. I stood up and exposed my tackle to the rush hour traffic.

The bus had left, and I was left – humiliated - sitting in my own excreta, tackle exposed, wondering how the hell I was going to wipe my bottom.

King Juan Carlos meets Dracula

Food Glorious Food may have been a surprise hit from the early 70s - much loved musical - Oliver, but not in darkest, communist Romania in 1982.

Food, what food?

Ceausescu built the biggest palace of any potentate on the planet. I'm sure he boasted in meetings - with other leaders of the Warsaw Pact in dimly lit rooms behind the Iron Curtain - "Mine is bigger than yours". Of course it was, he had to spend the national wealth of the nation on something, and it certainly wasn't on infrastructure or feeding his people. So, when you have spare billions in your current account, unaccounted for, why not get rid of it by building a huge pad for yourself. I think they call it 'trousering'

Ceausescu's personal favorite song from Oliver was Fagin's hit: *You've Got To Pick A Pocket Or Two.* He took the advice literally - and stole money off everyone in Romania.

The shops in Bucharest in 1982 were completely bare. The only food I found in large quantities, were jars of pickled gherkins, bread and tins of pilchards in tomato sauce. So unless you were a cat, or the chief gherkin buyer for McDonalds, Romania wasn't the place to be wined and dined. Probably still isn't.

I can't abide pilchards in tomato sauce. The best thing - in my opinion - is to bypass the digestive tract, open the tin, and pour it straight down the toilet. Save time by cutting out the middleman.

There are two things I hate more than pickled gherkins: speed bumps and Alan Carr in stand up. If I go to McDonald's, which is very infrequently, I have to remove the gherkin out of my Big Mac. I don't see the point of them, they make me bilious, and to be honest, I'm windy enough without it coming out both ends.

So, for my week in Bucharest, I went on an involuntary hunger strike, in the land that was a culinary wasteland. No wonder Dracula started drinking blood. He couldn't find anything else to sink his teeth into. – That's a fact.

I was so hungry, at one point I considered eating my own earwax or the fluff out of my belly button. I had heard that after a nuclear winter one of the only things to survive are cockroaches:

They can survive for two years at the bottom of a linen basket, by eating dust.

Truth was, I was wasting away, like Bobby Sands during his 'dirty cell' protest. They say man cannot live on bread alone, but as dull, and as stale as it was, I was forced to do so.

So when a local on the tram was tucking into a chicken wing, and some kind of dough ball soaked in vodka, I started to drool like Clement Fraud's dog. I couldn't take my eyes off him. The drooling left an embarrassing damp patch in the crotch of my beige trousers.

I looked like one of the cast from *One Flew Over The Cuckoo's Nest*. He noticed me and my expanding wet patch, smiled and offered me a piece of chicken and the alcohol soaked bread.

It was only after I'd eaten it, that I realized, I

should have stuck to pilchards in tomato sauce. The chicken was 'on the turn' and raw in places. If not raw, cold enough to suggest I would be in for a spot of 'trouble' later. The vodka-bread-balls were far too strong for my delicate western palate, if indeed it was vodka - it tasted like paraffin.

Some hours later – you've guessed it - I found out, the chicken had indeed been raw, and it was - as I had expected - paraffin. It certainly went through me like paraffin.

I found out that the Eastern Block, prior to 1990, used to pick their women's Olympic shot putting team from a shoddily dressed bunch of Romanian toilet attendants.

The female attendant guarding the public toilets - as vehemently as Cerberus, the three headed hound guarding the gates of hell was no beauty. Even in porcine circles - the term 'lipstick on a pig' would have been apt.

If Cerberus had been a nanosecond longer dispensing the bog roll, Bobby Sands would not have been the only one sitting in a dirty room.

My Romanian wasn't up to much, certainly not

fluent, but I got the message, she was in no hurry to let me passed, unless I crossed her paw with silver.

I was so close to the toilet, I had inadvertently 'relaxed', and being pinned up at the shit house door - by a person of indeterminate sex, with a grip of steel - did nothing to arrest my urge to 'spread the load'.

I was absolutely frantic, searching through my saliva stained trousers with one hand, whilst gripping my sorry buttocks with the other. I couldn't hold out any longer, I screamed like a banshee "Let me go, can't you see I'm about to shit myself?"

I did note that the floor had been recently mopped, and she may put me in a death choke, should I spoil it.

I threw two silver coins at her, but to be fair, I'd have happily parted company with a £50 note, just to feel free of the terrible burden I was temporarily carrying.

She accepted the coinage, in fact, she smiled, so I knew I'd given her far too much, In return, she unravelled the toilet roll and gave me, what I considered to be, far too little. In fact, a single shiny poor quality sheet, the thinnest I'd ever seen. I'd blown bubbles of fairy liquid with thicker membranes.

I looked at her in disgust, what good was that to anyone I thought, as I turned and gave it toes to the nearest cubicle.

As I 'pebble dashed' the pan, I pondered my predicament. How to make the best use, of a single sheet of toilet paper?

Origami was not something I was particularly good at, but I doubt a Japanese expert could have made a 'flapping bird' out of a single sheet of Romanian bog paper.

I feared it was 'brown finger nail' time.

But wait, perhaps not.

I remembered in my rucksack, I had an old map of Spain. On one side, was the complete Iberian Peninsula, and on the other, was a photo of King Juan Carlos.

I will say, that by the time I had finished wiping, the motorway network through Spain had been hastily extended, and a new, extremely wide highway ran from Madrid all the way past Barcelona, into what can only be described as land reclaimed from the Mediterranean.

On the other side of the map, most alarmingly, I had inadvertently given his majesty – King Juan Carlos of Spain, what is commonly known as, a 'dirty Sanchez'.

Flying by the Seat of your Pants

As 1985 drew to an inevitable close, and the world partied, at the stroke of midnight, I was in the toilet at Dhaka International airport, stroking my backside for the very last time that year. A minute later, I was still mercifully cleaning myself up for the very first time of 1986.

In an act, similar to crossing the *international date line*, in the middle of the Pacific, I had managed, totally unintentionally, but no less impressively, in a small toilet cubicle in Bangladesh - to straddle a period of two years in a single movement. A bowel movement!

The poster in Rangoon's travel agents read:

"Fly Biman - The better you know Bangladesh"

This is a totally misleading statement, and could be challenged in a court of law by any half decent defamation lawyer, to be libel.

It should have read:

"Fly Biman – You should know better"

This would be nearer to the truth. We departed terra firma in Dhaka, in a fashion modelled to that of a Harrier Jump Jet, and seemed to glide into Calcutta. The pilot had the misfortune of flying the most unreliable aircraft engine in the Commonwealth.

Arriving in Calcutta - in the same style we had left Dhaka - on the back of an airborne 'Big Dipper ' – vertically - we fell onto the runway from what must have been a hundred feet. For a moment we were airborne again, and then the pilot, who I am sure had little more than an international drivers licence, and was only in the captain's seat, due to winning an obscure Bengali television show, along the same lines as our very own *Jim'll Fix It*, proceeded to impress everyone on board with his aerial tomfoolery - attempting a second landing on his front wheel.

He stopped a little too abruptly for everyone's liking, to a crescendo of blood curdling screams, from the passengers, and Dum Dum Air traffic control tower, at the end of a 10,000ft runway, with only inches to spare.

The pilot was out of his depth, and was forced

to call for assistance to be towed backwards to the terminal.

I am sure, the aircraft manufacturers McDonnell Douglas - would have been horrified at the man's blatant disregard for a superb piece of mechanical machinery.

Just as certain, Evel Knievel would have taken his hat off to the man for his nerves of steel.

Turn Left at Biffins Bridge

Cycling is fun, but only if you live in Holland or on the Bolivian Salt Pan, and let's face it, only necessary if you are strapped for cash and can't afford either a motorbike or a car. It is at those moments in your life that you begin to recall your teacher's comment: To pay more attention in class. Well, guess what sunshine? It might have helped you get a better job later on in life, you waster!!!

There is no sight that grates more than being piss wet through waiting for a bus, when the school nerd drives past in his Bentley GT. Point taken!

I hadn't been on a bike in ten years. I wasn't actually sure I would still be able to find it in the garage, under the mountain of boxes of unwanted ornaments and old *Top Of The Pops* volume 17 LPs I was hoarding in the garage.

All teenage boys know the mysterious pelvic pleasure of finding 70's Top Of The Pops album covers at the bottom of your dad's HiFi cabinet. Everyone's personal pre pubescent favourite: The *Gratton's* catalogue.

Pages 71–79 inclusive: Ignoring ladies dressing gowns and full corsets – Grandma style.

The bike in question was an extremely cheap mountain bike called KILIMANJARO. That was where the relationship between mountain and bike ended.

This particular mountain bike was so poorly constructed it had trouble getting over speed bumps, let alone going up hills.

I noticed that when I sat on it, I was a little close to the ground, and that the wheels were a little small, and the tyres too fat and chunky. Images of those horrible clowns at the circus, cycling along on tiny bikes to pre recorded laughter, springs to mind. A pet hate of mine: Clowns.

I decided that the best thing to do - before my cross Britain dash - was to take it to the local bike shop for a service.

The shopkeeper was a sarcastic Scouser. As we all know, everyone born within the city limits of 'Scouseland' is by birth rite sarcastic, and proud of it. Anyway, the bloke could not help it, when he asked me: "What is that, this is a bike shop?" I foolishly told him I was about to cycle across Britain on it.

The high pitched whistling noise coming out of his nostrils - as he tried to curtail a laugh - had dogs all over Anfield barking mad.

"Mate, Cycle across Britain? I wouldn't cycle to the shops on that". He added with an element of bemusement "That's a child's bike"!! I had thought, even to my vertically challenged stature, it was rather low.

He tried to convince me to part with 500 pounds on a new bike, but I thought, perhaps a little too abruptly "Sod it, I'll show him. I'm going on the KILIMANJARO". And did....

I turned up at my mate's house totally unprepared.

Dressed in a Tony Hawkes skateboarding helmet, that had brought jeers from a crowd of 'no marks' hanging around a bus shelter. I had almost fallen off, when I narrowly avoided a parked car, as I attempted to turn and give the 'two fingered' salute to them, as they shouted "The kip of him".

As we set off, the others asked how much water I was carrying in my rucksack. They all had CAMELBAKS, I said "What water?" They asked, "So why is your rucksack so heavy"? They had gathered it weighed a lot, as every time I went around a bend, I leaned like Barry Sheen at *Silverstone*.

I opened it and showed them: A pack of Kendal mint cake, and an economy size bottle of Listerine mouthwash.

We were cycling from Morecambe to Scarborough and it was going to take three days.

Cycle across the Pennines, with a chest infection, no water, but a lovely fresh feeling in my mouth, - the minty taste lasted all day.

The taste did, but unfortunately I didn't. The lack of hydration took its toll, and I fell behind after thirty miles. I was wobbling erratically, almost delirious.

I fell off after three miles when we stopped abruptly and I forgot to take my foot out of the pedal straps. Falling into a bramble bush, silently, like a cunning fox after a hare. I slid into a barbed wire fence. Cut to ribbons, stung by nettles, pinned to the fence, I crucified myself, as I somehow managed to get the barbed wire, stuck behind my ear.

The rain came down like pencils, in a biblical torrent, my panniers snapped and I was forced to cycle the remaining 160 miles with it held in place with a piece of string. All in all I was a sorry looking sight.

By the end of day one, just out of Settle I was in a terrible state. My Tony Hawkes skateboard helmet looked like a disco ball there were so many dried sweat crystals embedded in it.

Every evening, as I rubbed my extremely tender scrotum, my dad would phone to ask how it had gone and to ask my whereabouts. He had been monitoring our progress on the Internet, via an ordinance survey map.

By day three my 'Biffins Bridge' was in a right mess. My gel seat did little to ease the abject pain of every revolution of the wheel.

My arse, and particularly my sack, swelled up to an alarming, if somewhat, pleasing size. To be hung drawn and quartered would hurt less. 'Biffins' was weeping, and so was I, as we relentlessly pushed on.

As I pedalled into Scarborough resembling a cast member of Schindler's List - Arsehole in tatters, my perineum weeping, like a teenager who had just been dumped by her first love.

The train journey home to Liverpool was a godsend - welcome relief. My bum had been through the trenches. I gingerly stepped off at Lime Street station and limped to the local platform for BroadGreen, weary but triumphant.

My dad called and said: "Where the hell did you go? I followed you as far as Biffins Bridge and I couldn't find it anywhere. I have no idea where it is? Is it the other side of Bridlington?"

I told him it was closer than he thought!!.

When I told him what I meant, when I had said: "Day three is a lot easier, but Biffins Bridge is in a terrible mess", he laughed.

However, it was a good few weeks before I laughed again. My scrotum scabbed up something awful. And, for a month, I made a General Hogmanay Melchett style "Oh ah" noise, every time I eased myself into a chair.

I haven't cycled since, but I am pleased to announce: Biffins Bridge made a full recovery.

Bored Shitless

Everyone knows what it is like to attend an extremely dull meeting, especially in IT, which seems to attract more than its fair share of very serious, earnest individuals. The sort of people you would not like to be set adrift in a lifeboat with.

Indeed, if I ever had the double misfortune of firstly crashing into the sea, and secondly, after surviving the impact, find myself stuck in a small craft with a group of IT geeks, I would probably jump out and take my chances with the sharks, or wait until nightfall, and eat them one by one.

At one such 'workshop' the subject matter was Mainframe Encryption. A subject matter so dull and so complex, that Einstein once did a talk on it, and dosed off mid sentence.

The room was full, there must have been twenty people sat around the boardroom table, and only two people had a clue what was going on.

Looking around the room, I noticed everyone was nodding and smiling in the right places, but they were all thinking about their holiday entitlements, or the burst water pipe at home. They certainly weren't thinking about the question at hand.

The bloke opposite me put his hands to his chin, as though he was praying, in a statement that said, "Let me consider that a moment", when I knew, he was "bored shitless". I certainly was.

In truth, the same bloke told me, only the day before, that World War 2 ended in 1985!! So how he thought he could pull the wool over everyone's eyes - and have everyone in the room believe he knew about Mainframe Encryption, when in truth, he probably had trouble spelling it - is any one's guess.

As one hour, dragged into two, time seemed to stand still, like a day on Venus. People actually started reading the words on the fire alarm. They started to take an interest in the air conditioning vents. They started counting the roof tiles on the ceiling. They did anything, but concentrate on the subject matter. It wasn't that they didn't want to know about Mainframe Encryption, they just couldn't grasp its complexity.

It was like trying to teach quantum physics to a four year old.

No one wanted to be there, and as the two and a half hour mark passed - without so much as a toilet break - fidgeting started.

It was not worth clock watching, as when clock watching, the fingers never seemed to move. Like the clock tower in the memorial garden in *Hiroshama,* we were stuck in this meeting room for all eternity.

There seemed to be a lot of shifting in seats; doodling on notebooks; a lot of yawning uncontrollably, and that was just the bloke leading the meeting. To be honest, I had wanted the toilet for some time, and had been shifting in my seat for a good hour and a half. People started to sneak the odd 'trouser cough', hoping everyone in the room would subconsciously blame the person sat next to them.

So it was with genuine delight when the meeting was called to a close. And like a rat escaping from a playful cat, everyone fled, mostly into the 'gents'.

I was so keen to empty my rather full bowel, that I committed the cardinal sin - A restroom 'no-no'. I didn't check for toilet paper!

As a satisfyingly dull thud hit the pan, I turned to unravel the roll. To my horror, it was empty.

My dad always said: "Life is like a toilet roll, at first it goes round very slowly, but at the end it whizzes around - far too quickly".

All that remained was the cardboard roll. I really was stuck.

My 'pollards' streaked the porcelain, and the last thing I needed was marble-effect underwear. I considered shuffling from one booth in to another - trousers around my ankles - but knowing my luck, the IT Director would walk in.

I had an idea. I waited until everyone had gone out of the Gents, and then I phoned my mate with my mobile, and explained my predicament. After he had stopped laughing, he obliged and I heard the Gents door open, he walked over to the cubicle next to me.

He let out a slightly amusing, but genuine " Phoar!!"

He said "You owe me for this". Under the cubicle came the ultimate hand of friendship - he proceeded to hand me sheets of *Andrex* - one at a time, and to add to my embarrassment, waited for me to wipe and beg for more.

As we left the toilet, he turned to me and said it had sounded like a cat was doing its business in the cat litter...

Charming!!!!

FOOTNOTE – For the bloke who thought the second world war ended in 1985, the reason I added the comment about a day on Venus, is because remarkably a single day on Venus lasts longer than its actual year. It is pointless me trying to explain, you will not understand.

Just nod knowlingly!!

Set it Free

I really do admire security guards. They have made a career out of doing absolutely nothing.

The only other people with more time on their hands are prisoners. So, how lazy are Prison guards? People with nothing to do, watching people, with even less to do.

You often see security guards, feet up, reading a 'very well read newspaper. Or watching TV, eating chocolate digestives, sipping endless mugs of tea, and whispering into *walkie-talkies*: "Everything is okay here".

Of course everything is OK. They only need a pair of pyjamas and they would be ready for bed.

But; Lets face it - If there were no security guards, there would be an increase in crime, therefore, more prisoners, and an exponential increase in the number of prison guards – thus, an endless cycle of nothing.

The way very clever scientists describe the eons before the 'Big Bang'. All that research money has been wasted, they could have spent a fiver on research, then proclaimed – We need more prison guards. Job done.

When I arrived back from Australia, I needed a job. There was very little mainframe computer work, in 1992.

I went for an interview at the famous shipbuilders, on the banks of the Mersey. To be honest, I didn't really impress at the initial interview. When they asked how I would put out an electrical fire I suggested a water hydrant!! I was very nervous, and actually meant to say foam, but that was wrong also.

I know the saying 'three strikes and out', but at the shipyard in those days, three strikes a week was normal. So, rather surprisingly, I got the job.

Next thing I know - I'm sitting in a porta-cabin on the basin wall - looking out over the Mersey - reading a newspaper, eating biscuits and drinking gallons of tea.

The shipyard was refitting a Royal Fleet Auxiliary ship, and my contract would last four months. Four months of gorging myself - I feared I'd end the contract looking like a walrus in a hard hat.

We designed a rota that meant we patrolled the 1,000 ft vessel constantly - mainly to stop us from overdosing on Kit Kats, and burn off the excessive number of calories we were consuming.

Mountaineers climbing K2, consume fewer calories in a day.

The ship was a hive of inactivity during the day, as everyone had union duties to attend to, but resembled the 'Marie Celeste' at night.

On one such night shift I was patrolling the bow of the ship - near the Captain's quarters - when I was 'caught short'. I knew it was a good ten minutes to walk off the ship and over to the security hut, so I made a tactical judgement: When you have got to go, you just have to go. I told my colleague - the biscuit eating *pinniped* - to keep an eye out.

There was no need - people crossing the Antarctic solo saw more people than us on board at night.

I went to the Captain's 'Heads', and in the words of Captain Kirk: "The Captains log, star date 1992 – Uranus"

As the Captain's log came into this world for the very first time, its life was cut short by cries from my colleague, alerting me to the fact this part of the ship, hadn't been plumbed in yet.

Merseyside has launched a host of famous vessels over the years. And now I was going to 'slide a brown' down the slips. How appropriate, that in this famous shipyard, I too, had launched my own 'floater'.

I looked behind me at my sorry stool, struggling in the waterless pit, like a lungfish caught between swampy ponds in the unforgiving African heat of the dry season. I knew there was only one thing for it.

I found a plastic bag and made a makeshift glove, scooping my helpless friend to safety from a perilous end. At that point the words of Rolf Harris came to me: "Did You Think I Would Leave You Dying"

I ran through the corridor, and as my colleague shouted after me: "That is one big turkey", with the unconditional love a father feels for his child, I reluctantly and a little tearfully, flung my 'spendings' over the side and into the river.

It was free, born free, as free - as the wind blows!

My Mersey Goldfish had a fighting chance. It may even return one day, like salmon around the globe, fighting against the strong eight knot current, to breed in the murky, frigid waters of Birkenhead.

Red Alert!

For those with lycanthrope hairlines, a luxuriant head of hair can be a curse. Like a badger with fleas, you can end up looking remarkably unkempt. The Lord Mayor of London is a case in point.

From the neck down, you can tell he is 'rolling in cash', but sadly, from the neck up, he looks like he has been dragged through a hedge backwards.

No form of grooming can mask his disheveled appearance. That's what too much hair can do to a man.

I would say that of course, as I have very little of it myself - hair, or cash - for that matter!

So, whoever invented Brylcreem, I take my hat off to you.

Some extremely rich people use the product, well perhaps not use it, advertise it, maybe more appropriate. As a result they are handsomely rewarded for doing so.

I unfortunately paid a very heavy price for using the damn stuff. I suppose you could argue it was my own fault. Fool hardy, some might say.

On the day I left to go around the world, I had the fiscal misfortune of changing my money when the dollar to pound sterling ratio reached a historic, all time low. One pound bought just one dollar three cents.

Donald Trump look out, I'm behind you.

As a result, I didn't have much cash to play with and I hadn't even left our shores. To say I had to be frugal was an understatement. Buying stuff in *Pound Land* was as frivolous as eating truffles on a bed of saffron.

So, when a bloke in a pub told me a money saving idea, to avoid buying expensive branded sun cream - I listened intently. It did sound feasible that the reason all taxi drivers appear to have very brown necks, is due to the excessive brylcreem they use in their hair.

Funnily enough, I had noted that on a recent ride in a taxi, the driver had a neck George Hamilton III would die for.

That was my downfall, as I stepped out, on to

the beach, on the Croatian Island of Brac, armed with little more than a snug fitting pair of 'budgie smugglers' and my sun factor minus twenty, economy tub of Brylcreem. I was asking for trouble. I mean - Who the hell wears 'budgie smugglers' these days?

I can report, it went on beautifully smooth, if a little greasy.

Twenty minutes of zero cloud cover in temperatures hovering around 35 degrees Celsius - I had started to notice a slight reddening around my shoulder, five minutes later it became a tingle.

Half an hour later, I sensed a slight electrical burning smell on the wind, but put it down to a man selling lamb kebabs close by.

When I woke up two hours later, I quickly realized, the burning smell had been me. Christ Almighty, I was blistering like a tar pit. Only the lord could save me now. Even my chest hair had been singed.

The only place on my whole body, that didn't resemble a ripe, juicy plum tomato, was, oddly enough - my plums.

I burned like a witch on trial. The Kuwaiti oil

fields generated less heat, when the Iraqi's set fire to them, as they retreated back over the border in 1990.

My nose, well, what nose? I looked like, a melting ice- cream cone, that a child had dropped on the pavement, on a particularly hot day.

I ran for the shade of a nearby umbrella, as my friend called for assistance.

I shivered like a wet dog on top of *Helvellyn,* whilst the kebab seller called for an ambulance.

As the crowds dispersed, and the sun sank below the horizon, a glorious sunset was replaced by the rising moon. In a never-ending game of galactic billiards, I was emitting a strange luminous green hue - reminiscent of the melt down in the core reactor of a nuclear power station.

Thinking the green light in the sky may be a rave – several people began to party.

As I waited for the air ambulance to fly me to the mainland, I sat there like one of the patients in 'The Awakening' – unable to speak, too sore to muster even a smile, but my mind was alert and racing – I could not stop thinking about the taxi driver and his lovely tanned neck.

I knew what I'd do if I ever saw him again – I'd say – "If you want a tip mate, I'll give you a tip - keep that neck away from me or I might just ring it"

The Great Escape

I had heard that women who live together, on occasion, fall in line with each other, in the cyclic ladies department. But it is most unusual for blokes who share a flat, to want a crap at precisely the same time. It is even stranger, for them to have - a synchronized, ugly bout of diarrhoea.

Like a referee and his assistant, attempting to synchronize watches at the start of a Premier League game - the drama unfolded!

We put it down to one of two things: A bad pint or two, or, more likely, the dodgy clam chowder we had eaten the night before.

I thought at the time, it wasn't the warmest soup I'd ever eaten, and sadly the clams were more like frozen prawns. The net result was, we had the trots on a campsite outside of Toronto. And 'trot' we did, to and fro to the campsite toilet block. On this occasion, we galloped like *Aldaniti*, and arrived in unison.

Even though we were very good friends, pooing in public, is a touchy subject. There was an awkward pause as we looked at each other, hesitated and nodded, as though we were gladiators entering the arena. For most blokes, a good crap is a private affair - a LOVE affair - and the last thing you need is a gooseberry in the cubicle next door.

I chose trap one and he chose trap three. We left trap two empty. It was purely a psychological divide - an imaginary line, -like the tropic of Capricorn - it was only four feet, but it made a difference.

However, Four feet did not make the slightest difference to the acoustics. There was a 'Noah's Ark' of amusing animal noises, coming out of trap one and three. At one point it sounded like a bird of prey had flown through the open window, and my mate was having a fight with a Barn Owl, whilst trying to crap at the same time.

We obviously did our best to deaden the sound. You know the drill: Toilet paper on top of the water; shift buttocks to left and right, so the offending 'Tommy' will hit the porcelain first and break its fall, so it slips silently into the murky water. Anything to stop the ultra embarrassing SPLOSH noise we all hate. The aftermath which follows: Usually in the form of back wash - from the 'Barnes Wallace' bomb -

which spills up and wets your arse, is always upsetting , if always expected.

Every time I create an amusing SPLOSH, I bite my lip, and it was the same then. I bit my lip to stop myself from laughing.

A man came into the GENTS and seeing one and three occupied, he helped himself to trap two. The poor bloke must have had the same clam chowder as we'd eaten!

A whole lot of coughing, sniffing, heavy breathing, and then he let out the most god awful scream; not dissimilar to a soldier who has been shot, and is getting the lead shot pulled out of his chest with a pair of tweezers.

He unleashed hell - Followed by a slight whimper, as though he was pining for something. After a slight pause came the lull before the storm. Bracing himself, just like residents on the East coast of the United States, awaiting the arrival of a category five hurricane, he prepared for the worse - Boy – it never rains, it pours!

What came next can only be described as the opening scene from *Saving Private Ryan*. Absolute carnage!!

As he let out various oh's and ah's we listened in quiet reverence, aware that we were witnessing something special, we were in the presence of ' thunder box' greatness.

He was in 'Throne room' Nirvana!! To us mere mortals he was a 'lavatorial god'.

We couldn't help ourselves. We burst out laughing!!

He shouted: "Hey – what's going on?" We laughed even louder. He then said: "Just you wait till I wipe my arse, then I'll wipe the floor with you!"

With the threat of an imminent 'good hiding' hanging over us, we very swiftly, but not totally convincingly, wiped our own arses. We slipped silently out in to the night, like our 'turtles head' had moments before.

Ride into Hell

I do accept that it was rather late when I arrived in Karachi, and the bus into the city had probably stopped running.

But to try and charge me thirty dollars - a man's wages for a month - did seem rather high. No matter how hard I tried to haggle with the blanket-clad rabble, I couldn't get them to drop the price.

I was in a city of ten million, it was the other side of midnight - I hadn't a clue where I was, they had me over a barrel. If I'd refused to pay they could have taken me down a side alley, and actually put me over a barrel. So, I reluctantly paid.

I climbed aboard the 'Tuk-Tuk', and a young impertinent local, slid in beside me.

He introduced himself. What the hell was he doing in my taxi? I placed my rucksack between us for good measure.

He began on a helpful note. He lived in Karachi, and he warned me there were a lot of bad people living in the city, that would want to take advantage of a westerner alone. He was at the top of my list of those people that might try.

He smiled a sinister 'Dick Dastardly' type smile. It sent a shiver down my spine. He praised himself as being an honest man, and said that he would help me all he could, which was fine if I'd needed it, but I didn't. As I had suspected all along, he was the biggest cheat west of the Ganges Delta.

We arrived at an extremely low budget, well it can only be described as a hovel, but he called it a 'guesthouse'. The foyer was open to the street, and it had, without a shadow of a doubt been recently condemned. The rug hadn't seen a vacuum cleaner since *Ghengis Khan* rode through on his way to *Xanadu*.

The cost of the room, was again, a rather convenient - thirty dollar. Thirty dollars could have bought the plot of land the hotel sat on.

This was supposed to be a budget trip. In the last hour, I was spending money like Heads of State. I did manage to talk the 'hotelier stroke slob' down to 25 dollars - if I stayed two nights. Take my bank details, empty my account - you heartless thieving git.

I was escorted to my open plan, by that I mean - open to the elements bedroom, by an overtly feminine looking chap. These days I think they refer to them as *lady boys*, but in 1986 I had never seen a *'chick with a dick'*. Still haven't, I might add.

In those days *gay* meant happy, and the closest I'd been to a bloke who acted like my sister, was watching Dick Emery on Saturday nights.

I could hear my new taxi buddy babbling on in Urdu with the hotelier, no doubt negotiating a hefty commission.

Suddenly the biggest cheat in Pakistan came into my room, without so much as knocking - helped himself to the only chair, and pouring himself a glass of water, with the familiarity of a husband and wife. He began to speak, and it was then that he made his motives clear.

He made it sound as though, I was missing the chance of a lifetime. He would be my guide during my stay in Karachi, and he would haggle for me, look after me, and watch my back. I could throw in the meals, and all for fifty dollars. He didn't look like he had earned fifty dollars since the day he was born. At this suggestion; my face went a brilliant, flame red.

I was furious, the man's cheek knew no bounds. I asked him to leave, but he just stood there. To make matters worse, a group had gathered at the door and started to giggle. He began with the cocksure attitude of OJ Simpson's attorney.

He started by saying I was an unreasonable man. He continued to slur my character by saying he had tried to bargain down the price of my taxi - when in truth - he was one of those who had tried to charge me thirty dollars in the first place! The hard sell came next.

He started a tearful tale, and insisted I give him some cash, as his children were hungry, and one of them needed a life saving operation. When I kept saying: "Bugger Off", he turned nasty, said I had wasted his time and that he should have stayed at the airport and waited for a plane full of Americans.

This was the final straw, as my already flame red face turned an alarming puce. I yelled loudly and pinned him up against the wall. I said I'd rip his rudimentary 'testes' off if he didn't leave. He protested that he was a very poor man. I shouted it was better to be poor than crippled. Sensing I'd had enough of him - and I might turn nasty myself - he left, Urdu expletives ringing in my ears.

Left alone in my room - surrounded by all the domestic squalor, it was a good ten minutes before my face returned to its normal shade. Indeed, at one stage, I feared I would remain purple for good.

Terry Waite's Allotment

Whilst waiting for the second part of Monday night's *Coronation Street,* my girlfriend gave me the remote.

I started going through the programmes I had recorded on Sky Plus.

One of the programmes was Ross Kemp's *Extreme World.* I don't like him, but I like seeing him crap himself when interviewing hardened criminals in prison. He acts very tough, but if it all kicked off, he would be first back to the safety of his 'on set' caravan. He would wait until the coast was clear, and then, after a quick change of underwear, he'd be back out, camera following his every move.

Ross Kemp was in Beirut in this particular episode, I was in Beirut in 2003, and it was a great place to visit. Everyone was really friendly, but the locals complained that nobody ever went there, mainly because, ten years after the fighting had finished, it still had the 'war torn' image.

I mean, ok, the buildings are pock market

with bullet holes and parts of the city have not been rebuilt. But when I think about Pompeii, It is still a ruin, and Vesuvius has been dormant for centuries. You don't go on a day trip from Naples thinking you are going to be covered in a burning dust cloud. So why steer clear of Beirut?

My girlfriend was totally disinterested in the programme. She was more concerned about Deidre and Ken's marriage problems. However, to be fair, she sat through it, but with a face on her like a wet weekend.

Ross Kemp was in the area where Terry Waite was kidnapped, so I turned to her and said: "It must have been terrible", she said: "What was terrible?" I replied: "You know, Terry Waite held in captivity for five years, in a room on his own, chained to a radiator ".

Her response was priceless. She turned to me and in a very serious voice said: "Was it on?" I said: "Was what on?" She said: "The radiator", in a voice that suggested I was the stupid one.

I couldn't believe it!

I was slightly sarcastic with my retort, "How the hell do I know, and to be honest, that would be the least of his problems".

She then said: "Well, I wouldn't be able to". I said in disbelief: "Be able to what?"

She started to get irritable herself at this point - "Be held in captivity if the radiator if it wasn't switched on, especially in winter, it would be freezing"

As if she would have a choice...

I couldn't help the rant that followed: "Well, next time we're holidaying in the Middle East and four armed men stop our taxi and bundle us into the boot of a waiting car, blind folded. I shall remember to ask them nicely, if they wouldn't mind taking the chill off the room before we arrive, as my girlfriend is a bit nesh."

She didn't speak to me for the rest of the night. In fact, she went to bed, with a face that resembled a wet bank holiday in Cromer. Bloody Ross Kemp!! He should change the series title to 'Ross Kemp - extreme domestic violence'.

So out of spite I turned the heating off.

By the time I went to bed a few hours later, I was blue with cold!!! I didn't tell her, but she was right.

In the scouts they always say be prepared, so I have taken the liberty of writing a note in both Arabic and French, stating in advance: I understand their reasons for wanting to take us hostage, but could they leave the radiator on in our cell. I shall pass the note to our captures, just prior to being blindfolded, should we be hijacked, whilst holidaying at some point in the future.

I can use it as a bargaining tool perhaps.

Brasilians are shite

Isn't it strange the way the Americans and English speak in a common tongue, but in so many ways, we don't know what each other is on about?

Ribald words, that to us are amusing, do not have the same impact, on the other side of 'The Pond'.

I am of course, referring to the word fanny. In New York, it means bottom, lots of Americans have enormous 'fannies' even the blokes. You see, its funny already – that's where it starts to get complicated, doesn't it.

A bloke with a fanny – good grief, surely not! I hear you say! Here in the UK, that's someone 'pre op!' But in the USA, there are one hundred and fifty million blokes with 'fannies'. In fact everybody in America has a fanny. Half of them have knobs as well. That makes them hermaphrodites doesn't it?

Now my mind is like Swiss cheese. You get my point! Extremely confusing – we are supposed to speak the same language!

In the UK and America, we both use the word shit, but if you say shite to an American, it doesn't mean anything. It doesn't exist in their vocabulary.

So, imagine the hilarious soccer commentary - from an American sports reporter - when I watched a soccer match in New York.

I forget who was playing, but they always seem to have odd nicknames for their professional teams.

It was something like the *Sacramento Willie Warmers*, playing the *San Jose Spanked Bottoms*.

Anyway, the thing I do remember was that a Brazilian player on the field was called Rafael Sheadt (Pronounced shite).

You would have thought that someone would have warned his mother before she married his father.

I mean, if I had a girlfriend and she found out my name was Buster Haemorrhoid, she wouldn't be my girlfriend for long. Not until I changed it to by deed poll to Aching Haemorrhoid .

With a name like that I'd be fighting them off with a shitty stick.

Rafael Sheadt (shite) was aptly named, because, he was!! He was the only Brasilian on the planet incapable of trapping a ball, or could pass it more than a few yards. Three toed sloths in the jungle move quicker.

As the game progressed, Rafael took a wild shot that went way over the crossbar. The commentator said: "And that was shite". Indeed it was!!

Later in the game, a tricky winger ran down the touchline, and without so much as smirking, he said: "He tried to turn, but he ran in to Shite"

The one that made me laugh the most was when he said of an opponent, "He had shite all over him".

A few years later, Rafael Sheadt turned up in Scotland. The weather matched his name I suppose.

He played for Celtic for a while, but they had the good sense to put RAFAEL on the back of his shirt.

However, everyone knew his surname, and opposing fans used to chant:

"You're Rafael and you know it"

Absolute Bliss!

Very occasionally, and I do mean only a few days per year, the conditions are right to perform the perfect stool. Of course it comes as an absolute joy to the recipient, as, like a bloke passing his driving test at the first attempt, it is totally unexpected.

There are no omens, no premonitions, not a sign that it will happen. You don't look out the window - see eleven magpies, and think, oh eleven magpies, that must mean the perfect bowel movement. It just happens!!

Most of the year, a bowel movement is mundane, functional, slightly dull, rather time consuming, and generally necessary. Unless of course, you have just won the lottery, in those circumstances you could afford to have an endless supply of underwear, and never wear them more than once. But even then, you would soon lose friends, if every time you met them, you smelled like the 'great London stink of 1858'.

On very rare days, when, like the happy accident that spawned life on earth, all the conditions are right, and at that exact moment, everything is in perfect harmony, it can be a wondrous experience.

Having a perfect poo is the mark of a true craftsman, like Michel Roux with his *soufflé*, it has to be baked to perfection. Leave it too long and the moment will pass. It may even retreat - like an army on the run - back up your 'jacksie'.

The consistency has to be just right, to facilitate an effortless movement. Not too soft, not too hard, there must be no corners on it, and it has to be as smooth as a ball bearing.

To add to the scatological bliss, you must arrive in the bathroom at precisely the right moment. A slight urgency perhaps, but none of the button popping desperate brow sweating kerfuffle, associated with yanking your trousers down, as you are in danger of a 'boil wash'.

Once out in the open, the cleanup has to be effortless in the backside wiping department, and a conservative use of toilet paper.

Only then can you start to believe you may get a perfect ten.

They say, the biggest telling off is the one you give your self. Let's be honest, self-analysis is a difficult thing. But to be content that you have done the utmost.

To leave no disappointment, no doubts in the back of your mind, that you did your best, and have left no turd unturned, there is one last test you must pass, literally!!!

In order to gain the Olympic qualification, you must produce the magical David Nixon - 'disappearing jobbie'. Like a free diver holding his breath, disappearing into the abyss. You must produce a turd, that under its own steam - that is the key criteria, under its own steam - no flush required. It slides silently unnoticed around the U- bend, leaving no trace, no 'pollards'. There must be no evidence you have ever been in the toilet.

The ghost poo is always a surprise. As you turn to take an affectionate look at all your handy work, sadly you find...like a son on his eighteen birthday – the turd has left, gone without so much as a "cheerio". I always find myself - at that point - saying those immortal words from the cartoon Deputy Dawg, when Musky says: "Where did he go? Where did he go??" as he rubbed his eyes in disbelief.

The only indication you have been to the toilet - like smelling burned toast in the kitchen, long after you've eaten it – is a familiar, yet rather unpleasant odour, that lingers in the bathroom and stings the nostrils..

The only blemish on a perfect score card is when someone shouts: "Christ – open the window!"

ABSOLUTE BLISS!!

Return to Sender

Sending a postcard should be an easy task. Let's face it, if mankind can put men on the moon, split the atom, and send photographs back from the outer reaches of our solar system - unless you were a pygmy in the Congo jungle or an Iban tribal warrior in a remote part of Borneo - posting a letter to a loved one, from anywhere in the world, should be pretty straight forward.

Not so. Try posting something in Pakistan. Its close proximity to India gives you a clue. Whatever you want to arrange, is going to be extremely long winded, time consuming, and utterly frustrating.

I only wanted to send one postcard to my parents, but it was like trying to organise a Rolling Stones concert in North Korea.

Taking a bus through the streets of Karachi, the bus was packed beyond capacity. People were sitting on the roof, on the bonnet, hanging off wing mirrors, even sitting on the driver's knee.

The bus was so overcrowded the driver was on another bus!

After three minutes the oxygen had all but been used up, and I was forced to breath in the rancid fumes of several camel- breathed locals, who probably hadn't cleaned their decaying teeth, or what remained of them, since Pakistan broke away from India in 1948.

In addition, I was subjected to the endless and deafening sound of everyone on board - coughing up phlegm, and clearing their throats of various colourful stews of uncertain substances.

Hindi music was being forced through a totally inadequate music system at 400 decibels, temporarily deafening everyone onboard. The vibrations from which had made everyone onboard completely sterile.

I was sent to four different building in temperatures close to 40 degrees Celsius, each building at least half a mile apart, when finally, totally by accident, I stumbled across another building, which happened to be the right one. Soaked in sweat, and as tense as

Andy Murray's tennis racket, I was dangerously close to having my first nervous breakdown.

Upon arrival at the correct post office, I was informed, by a surly gentleman - with an arse like a Bombay money lender - after he cleared his throat and spat on the floor, just missing my big toe - that I was in block D, and the post mistress in charge of European mail was in block G.

Arriving in block G, I was pushed from lengthy queue to lengthy queue, about five in all. By this time I was my now familiar colour – Puce!!.

Finally, thank the Lord, I was in the right queue, but people started to push-in, and from being third in line, I found myself at the back of a queue equal to any traffic jam on the M25 - on August bank holiday.

I was finally served two and a half hours after the horrendous ordeal had begun, not at all certain the postcard would leave the building, let alone arrive at my parent's house, six thousand miles away.

Just for the record... I sent the postcard in 1986 and it never arrived, but due to the inefficiency of every part of daily life in Pakistan, I am still hopeful, it might!!

Shitting through the Eye of a Needle

The only good thing about getting cholera was that whilst I had it, I no longer had amoebic dysentery. And whilst not quite as life threatening – It was absolutely draining, both physically and mentally. I couldn't trust myself, even the hint of a fart, It had me in a right *'two-and-eight'*. So having a bout of cholera was a godsend for both me, and the restaurant lavatory. Because, until my cholera was diagnosed, the toilets - like the open air swimming pool at New Brighton, in the gales of 1989 - had taken an absolute battering.

The fact I had cholera meant I had gone past the *sloople ploop* stage, as they say in Belgium. My body had actually given up alerting me to the fact I was about to shit myself. Indeed, it cut out the digestion process all together. It went straight from plate to pan.

It had started with a form of irritable bowel that seemed to manifest every Thursday. It wasn't actually an irritable bowel - it was, quite rightly - Absolutely fuming!

I had no idea what I ate on Wednesday's, but sure enough, every Thursday, I generally found myself, waiting for someone to finish in the only toilet in the building. Whilst waiting for patrons to vacate the bathroom, I had without realising it, perfected, a very crude Nepalese version of *River Dance*.

Dreading every Thursday, I knew by end of breakfast service I'd be shitting through the eye of a needle. One day it was so bad, I decided to save time, and eat my breakfast on the toilet.

I occasionally had a little accident, and in an attempt to avoid taking my underpants off - or taking the rest of the day off, I tried wearing two pairs of underpants. 'skiddies' was an accurate description. Having said 'little accident' no accident is little if you 'follow through', all hands on deck, high priority stuff.

'Following through' - when you are serving customers, can be problematic. After all, everyone eats with all their senses: Sight, taste, and of course smell. There is nothing more off-putting, to spoil the dining experience, as a bloke is just about to order cottage pie, than catching a whiff of my freshly tainted trousers, smelling distinctly RIPE!!

I was just in the process of taking a family of four's breakfast order, but sadly, I never got as far as writing down scrambled eggs.

 I got as far as writing SCRAMB... then my pen went down. I did, however, scramble myself, pretty sheepishly to the toilet. I backed off, apologising profusely as I retired. I never took another order. Writing the word SCRAMB was the last thing I ever did in that restaurant. An illustrious career cut short in its prime.

What I witnessed as I whipped off my trollies - in that small dark room, will haunt me for the rest of my life. Staring back at me in my sodden 'smalls', dangling precariously just below my 'mushroom-in-a-bale-of-hay' was the undigested porridge I'd eaten only an hour earlier, it had been expelled, just as it had been swallowed, hot and steaming, albeit, having rested in my guts for an hour, it was now slightly overcooked.

I thought the end had come. It was time to meet my maker. I thought I was going to die. I went to seek medical help immediately. Quick thinking and an equally quick diagnosis saved my life.

Sadly, nothing saved my under garments, not even two pairs had helped. Both had to be thrown away.

Later that day I looked out the window - a puppy had one pair on its head, and was tossing the second pair into the air with its extremely sensitive nose. It didn't flinch at the nasal stinging stench rising from my badly soiled Y fronts, as it tore them to shreds.

Those under garments had been with me ever since I'd left England. They had been at my side literally, every step of the way. We'd been through the good times and the bad. We had been through the 'loose' times as well as through constipation. Now they were confined to the great linen basket in the sky.

A tear welled up in my eye, it wasn't that I'd miss my 'under crackers', It was the stench emanating from what was perched on the end of the puppy's nose. I could smell it from the open window.

Surely that smell could only have been created by an alien life form. There were elements in my feculence that were not on the periodic table.

Scientists search for years to find such an abundance of new biological and chemical material to write about, and like the discovery of electricity, it was there all along, hidden, not so discreetly, thanks in part to the puppy, inside the badly soiled gusset of my underpants.

As for that puppy on the other 'paw' – It must have been as hard as nails, or more probable – lost its sense of smell!!

What a Dump!

Calcutta - Sunset over the Hugli River. Not exactly as inspiring as sunrise over Everest, but interesting to say the least.

They say Calcutta is a Black Hole, and it is in need of some TLC, but in a city of nine million, with a third of the population sleeping on the street, it is nothing short of fascinating.

The Howrath slums are on the southern side of the river, sitting, or should I say squatting, directly opposite Calcutta.

The problem with this part of the world is that even now, 27 years later, the vast majority of Indians have to poo *Al Fresco*. They do not have access to any toilet facilities at all.

That old nursery rhyme, S*kip, Skip, Skip To The Loo* was never more appropriate. On a boat trip down the Hugli, there were arses everywhere.

Row upon row of one eyed sentinels, lined the 'tommy' strewn riverbank. There were more rusty Sheriffs badges on show than in a Clint Eastwood *Spaghetti Western.*

Men, woman and children squatted side by side on the banks of the river, creating rivers of poo.

The stench in the air stung my enormous nostrils and as I watched one wretched individual living in a sewer pipe, and appeared to have a prolapsed colon - 'drop one' into the river.

I actually balked, from a hundred feet away.

The problem was, and probably still is - the Hugli is quite fast flowing. Great for those wiping there very exposed bums, but an absolute nightmare for those poor sods attempting to wash their faces thirty yards down stream.

At one point I looked across at the banks at one bloke crapping five feet away from another bloke who was cleaning his teeth.

"Hmm – What's that new toothpaste you're using today Sanjay? " "Oh do you like it, yes it's new – It's called hint of dog turd- the smell lasts 12 hours" .

"Well Sanjay I suggest you see a doctor, or a

dental hygienist at the very least."

So Sanjay makes an appointment to see the dentist , the following year, as he decides to waits until his remaining teeth fall out – then he would save money, by killing two birds with one stone.

"Excuse me doctor – I need a new set of dentures – Oh, and I have terrible bad breath, can you suggest anything for halitosis?"

"Yes – clean your teeth upstream you fool!!"

Peel a grape

Unless you came from circus stock, not many people can claim to be shot out of a cannon.

Fewer people can claim to have done what I did whilst bathing myself in Christchurch, New Zealand.

I had been to the beach and was covered in sand, so decided to have a bath. The place I was staying had a huge, old, cast iron bath.

As I sat there contemplating life, I could feel a touch of wind brewing. As there was no one about, I thought I would force a fart, just to see how loud it could be. Old bath, high ceiling, lots of tiles, floor and walls, the optimum conditions for noise reverberation - perfect for a "bum trump".

I really did peel one off. It was so loud I actually jumped. I remember my daughter trumping once so loudly it made her cry. Anyway, mine blew like a coronet player in a Cleo Laine jazz tribute. This was my own tribute - a rendition of 'The Last Post'!

My arse was talking to me - It appeared to say, quite distinctly: "What about a water bottle ". Don't pretend you don't know what I'm talking about it. We have all farted in the bath – forced an amusing trouser cough out. You probably laughed as you did it.

As I farted - well technically it is what we call in the trade - a 'dry shart' - something shot out of my bottom at quite a speed, and it actually hurt as it flew past my sphincter. Something made my eyes water!

"What about a water bottle"!! say it fast.

Raising an alarmed eyebrow, I looked down and saw a small grape. It was totally baffling. I couldn't remember eating a grape, or anything with grapes in it, since I left England. I was totally perplexed.

On closer inspection, the grape still had a stalk attached. No wonder it hurt - a small piece of wood ripping down my rectum, embedding splinters in my colon.

Then it dawned on me, it wasn't a grape at all, well I suppose officially it was. What had shot out my arse was a swollen sultana.

Then I remembered.   I'd had Mueselli for breakfast!!!

John Holmes Eat your Heart Out

Long, long ago, before Man Utd kept winning silverware, there existed an era called the English First Division. To some, and in particular Sky Sports, it never happened. Like *Pol Pot* and the Cambodian killing fields - year zero: Before which all records were obliterated from the history books.

It was a time, so long ago, that most cars still had wind- down windows. Electric windows were only for posh people. And an ashtray in a car was an optional extra, and people boasted that their car had headrests.

The year was 1992 and dinosaurs still roamed the earth. In those days it was perfectly acceptable to go out on a Saturday night, hit a girl over the head with a bit of four- by- two and take her back to your cave. " All above board your honour"!!

During this prehistoric period that my girlfriend invited her mother and brother for a six week holiday to England. They came with the princely sum of thirty pounds between them.

I wasn't a skinflint, but I was reluctant to take any of my extended family sightseeing, as it usually involved me spending large amounts of money. Especially when her brother started getting a taste for Guinness and Hagan Das ice cream.

I somehow ended up taking them to Knowsley Safari Park. I wish I hadn't bothered.

I have no idea what possessed her brother - who was sitting in the front passenger seat - to open the window. After all, it would be lunacy to go swimming if you could see a shark's fin in the water. Imagine - if a cobra started hissing at you, with its head bolt upright, no one would go over to it and flick it on the end of its nose.

This half-wit decided it might be a good idea to feed the elephants. Without asking, he wound down the window, and started throwing grapes at the nearest one to the car. As all animals do, it sniffed the ground and picked up the grape with its trunk.

We all thought it was a great idea - for about

ten seconds. Next thing the elephant gets the idea there may be food in the car. And to everyone's abject horror, steps forward, and puts its extremely long trunk through the open window, and starts sniffing for food in the car.

The nostrils were full of snot and dirt. To be honest I'd never seen an elephant trunk that close up, and could not believe how thick the hairs on its trunk were. They were like small chubby fingers.

In a blind panic the screams from everyone, particularly the half-wit in the passenger seat, who was frozen in fear and howling like a werewolf - were some of the most disturbing sounds I have ever heard. Some of them were not even human.

As the screams intensified the elephant sniffing got a little more localised. Unfortunately for my passenger, the area earmarked for sniffing, had moved to his groin.

The trunk suddenly swung from my now unsightly dashboard, to his pitiful, mucus-stained crotch. No doubt the elephant could smell fear. I could! And if the half-wit hadn't soiled his pants, he was certainly dribbling from the mouth, in a slightly gormless, and infantile way, as the Elephant continued to dribble uncontrollably, over his ever shrinking, terrified, and abused meat and two veg. If I wasn't screaming myself, I might have felt sorry for him. He had now reverted back to the womb, unable to perform even the most basic human functions. He had in the space of less than thirty seconds become a ' vegetable'

Whilst he had brought all this danger upon himself, no one deserves to be man handled by an elephant on the manhood.

The enormous beast's sniffing proboscis dangled inches from the floor. I am of course referring to the elephant's trunk, not his sorry genitals.

By now the screams were so loud they were drowning out the radio. He was so scared he reverted to swearing in Polish. My girlfriend said he was screaming: "God help my wretched testicles". Indeed, he was in a very serious predicament.

I was only grateful it wasn't my 'John Thomas' being molested by this monstrous mammal.

I did think about helping him by plucking a hair out of its nose, but I was frightened that might inflame the situation by annoying the beast.

If I had done that, it may turn on me and trample on my, as yet, unpaid for car.

So like the coward I was, I ignored his plea for help, and just screamed like a girlie!!

The shouting was so loud the baboons in the next field got agitated and started throwing their droppings at each other. To the other cars in the park, it must have seemed like the scene of a mass murder. I expect they were just glad it wasn't them.

Momentarily as the trunk extended from my brother- in- laws 'packet' I looked on with a mixture of resentment and envy at his new appendage: An eye wateringly impressive phallus, with a mind of its own.

I'm sure he could have got used to the 'John Holmes' look, If it wasn't for the mucus stained mess all over his trousers. I am not sure if the elephant had a cold, but the 'dew drops' falling from its enormous 'konk', were ruining my car.

The poor bloke sat beside me was frozen with fear. The screams had stopped, little more than an open mouth and silence was coming out of his terrified and contorted face.

He tried to scream but – nothing came out.

He had his hands to his face, and looked like *Monck's Scream.*

Time appeared to stand still, but the ordeal must have lasted less than a minute.

I turned to my girlfriend in the back seat, and screamed for her to throw some fruit out the window. She threw the rest of the grapes and a few bananas out onto the grass verge.

As quickly as it had begun, the elephant withdrew his offending trunk from the 'snot mobile', and started sniffing the fruit outside.

We wound the window up, as quickly as we could. We were mentally exhausted. We had been through a waking nightmare.

I know the signs in the park said: DO NOT EXCEED 10MPH, but I shot off so fast, I managed a skid mark on the tarmac. Like Alain Prost off the grid.

When we got home, we both checked our underpants for skid marks of our own, independently of course, but gave each other a clean bill of health. Unlike my car, it needed a full valet costing £40.

I haven't been to the Safari Park since!

You can tell me I'm a Doctor

You are never at your best 'down below', when you are a bit off colour, or you actually have to expose yourself in public. A mixture of both is called a trip to the doctors.

To add insult to injury, my trip to the doctor involved showing him my 'John Thomas' in too much detail for my liking. I needed to be circumcised but had not got the bottle to go and make an appointment.

My boss at the time was a bit of a playboy, who had a string of women. He said I couldn't go through life, scared stiff to go 'tatties deep', just because my foreskin was too tight. He said he would sack me, if I didn't make an appointment.

So, more alarmed that I might end up on the street, homeless and destitute, rather than loose the end of my 'todger', I found myself in the doctor's surgery. I was too scared to tell him what the trouble was. I made up a tale that I had been having sore throats for months. He examined me and was convinced I had tonsillitis, and perhaps I should have them removed. Little did he know it wasn't my tonsils that needed surgery!

I did think it was a rather poor show that the doctor had looked down my perfectly healthy throat, and suggested that I needed my tonsils out. He even wrote me a prescription for some medicine to sooth my inflamed windpipe. Absolutely amazing! I know the NHS have cut back in recent years, but really, if that is the calibre of student's we are recruiting into the profession, they should stay on the media studies course.

To be honest, if he was that bad at medical diagnosis, there was no way he was going to be let loose anywhere near my 'Tackle' with a knife. I could ill afford any slip up in that department. It isn't called a 'little man' for nothing!!

Almost convinced - I did have something wrong with my throat, I found myself thanking him, the fraudster, turned to walk out. It was only when I got to the door, I plucked up the courage to say: "Well actually doctor...."

Next thing I know, he's saying: "Let's have a look at it then"

As I started to unbuckle my trousers, I could feel my manhood disappearing into my body. It resembled a sliver of mincemeat. My 'Laddo' was rather shy to say the least. Nothing would coax it out from its hiding place, like a Moray eel hides in between the gaps in the coral reef.

I felt awkward and ashamed. If it withdrew any more, it would be the women's ward I'd be transferred to. Indeed, further shrinkage and I wouldn't need the operation, as I wouldn't have a manhood at all. It really had disappeared, like I'd jumped in a freezing mountain stream. It looked like one of those embryonic baby kangaroos, before they reach the safety of the pouch.

The doctor put on a monocle. I kept thinking it was a magnifying glass.

He then put my miniscule manhood on the end of his pencil. He raised an eyebrow and kept saying: "Hmmmmmm". Good job it wasn't a 6 inch rule. Okay you horrid little man – I thought – "Don't rub it in. Don't make it any more embarrassing than it already is – You could be kind and boost my confidence – Say something nice like - Wow!"

I felt like saying: "Get yours out then and see how smug you are". But I thought it might sound a little bit homoerotic.

Instead I was apologetic, and openly made a joke about the size, saying: "I bet you don't get many horses in here". At that point he furrowed his brow so tightly his monocle actually fell out onto the floor.

Inside I was shouting: "For god sake grow". I even tried to think of rude thoughts, but all I could think of was burning tyres and Margaret Thatcher!!!

Hovis – Great Bread – Terrible Bog Paper

In the days of General Tito's tenure at the helm, he impressively held together six, possibly seven (if you include Kosovo) nations with little more than an iron first and a loud, angry voice, and he called it Yugoslavia. In the recent past after all the fall- out in the Balkans, some people look back on his reign with rosy coloured spectacles.

I look back on my time in Yugoslavia with less than rosy coloured testicles, but with a fond nostalgia.

An inquisitive teenager, from the windswept North West of England, whose only previous chance, of seeing anyone with their top off at the beach, was seeing their uncle in a string vest, walking his dog along Prestatyn promenade on a partially warm day.

So suddenly to discover that raven headed beauties were prancing around in little more than Chanel No. 5 on sunny beaches 'abroad', was quite a thrill.

Indeed, Yugoslavia was 'abroad', and compared to everywhere I had been, it was hot and exotic.

All the blokes were tanned and wore heavy moustaches, with dark greased-back hair. It was the sort of place Brad Pitt would feel inadequate. He'd feel as handsome in Yugoslavia as Lyle Lovett. After holidaying in Yugoslavia 'The Pitts' would take to plastic surgery. Forget going home and unpacking – They would ask their driver to take them straight to a cosmetic surgeon.

They may have been handsome, but unlike 'The Pitts, Yugoslavs were not blessed with wads of cash, their wallets were as bare as: *Old* Mother *Hubbard's Cupboard,* and as a consequence, in order for them to feed their growing families, due to the fact, every northern European lady who set eyes on them, was pregnant half an hour after meeting them. They were all forced to work on the black market, to make ends meet. Everyone did 'things' on the side, to make extra dinars.

We had heard there was a nudist beach just around the headland, and if the beach we were on, anything to go by, there would be busloads of Eastern Europeans parading in the buff, frolicking like Yorkshire Terriers on heat. The two of us were rather keen to find out if this *Shangri la* existed.

The problem was, I didn't mind looking, but I didn't particularly want anyone to look at me, I certainly didn't want to 'drop my trolleys', and show the Yugoslavs, what put the 'Great' in Britain, because to be honest, it wasn't great at all.

The beach we wanted to go to could only be accessed via an extremely long walk, or by boat and beyond the headland.

Once there, it would be obvious we were not nudists. We were both worm white, and blistered on a sunny day in December. It was pretty obvious that our bodies hadn't been exposed in any way, shape or form, since birth.

So, we hired a canoe from a dashingly handsome, unkempt chap, with the most outrageous handle bar moustache, and equally outrageous - fake leather - bright red, crocodile skin boots - and a jumper that had seen better days. He must have worn it, everyday of Tito's reign, and hadn't washed it since. It was threadbare, and looked like a dog had got hold of the sleeve, and started to run down the beach with it in his mouth.

We crossed his grubby palm with silver, and paddled out to sea.

The tide and current was quite strong, and the headland was a little further than we had anticipated.

In no time at all, the great effort, the sun, the Yugoslavian goulash we had eaten at lunchtime, all started to take their toll.

A mile from the headland, and at least half a mile from the beach we had just left - in the middle of the Adriatic - I wanted a poo. I was in deep water, both metaphorically and actually.

I did think about 'launching' it over the side, but unless I had the poise and balance of Nadia Comaneci on the narrow beam, there was absolutely no way I could do my 'business' - without the canoe capsizing. I didn't fancy having to try and get back into the canoe in such deep water. I didn't really have the strength.

The only thing to do was head for the rocky islet about a hundred yards away. I wasn't sure what I would do when I got there, but at least it was terra firma. It may even offer a little bit of privacy, me the ocean, my mate, and a canoe.

By the time we got there I was ready to explode, like a suicide bomber.

I gingerly got out of the canoe and onto the rocky outcrop, and with much relief dropped my shorts.

My mate said he had no idea what I was going to clean myself up with. Neither had I. That scenario – wiping your bottom after going to the toilet! What an odd concept.

He only had a daypack, and we had little more than a few sandwiches. Regrettably, and a little fool hardy, I said: "That will have to do".

Next thing I know, as I'm swiping a cheese and pickle 'sarnie' across my own arse pickle, it fell apart into a million crumbs up my back passage.

My ring- piece looked like Andromeda, some far of galaxy.

To add to my plight, a seagull swooped down and pinched one of the sandwiches!!

In the end I was in a sorry state. Christ it was a mess, what a fiasco. It was as though someone had said to a three year old: "paint a picture of a house on that man's bottom"

I was stuck on a rock in the sea, arms out, covered in my own squalor, squatting like a cormorant drying its wings.

My 'dag' had got absolutely everywhere, even on my shoe. It was utter humiliation. It had been the worst idea since Kennedy said to his driver: "Turn left past that grassy knoll".

I had no pride left. I was absolutely spent. I had to rid myself of these apocalyptic 'dingleberries'.

I closed my eyes, looked to heaven and fell backwards into the sea, like an abalone fisherman. Arse and tackle in full view, as though watching some sort of weird pornographic baptism.

We never did see any nudists, but my mate did see my nether region - smeared in it's own 'doings' - do a perfect swallow dive into the crystal clear waters. In a matter of moments, the water quality dropped, and the nearest beach lost its blue flag rating!!

NOISY NEIGHBOURS

Many years ago, I opened a magazine and saw an advert that said: *Nepal – roof of the world, most people will only see it in an atlas.*

From that moment on, I knew I was destined to travel.

I lived in Kathmandu for four months, on the top floor of a block of flats, which I shared with an extremely eccentric American called Mr McKinney. He talked in riddles and only stopped for breath when he was in danger of passing out. He had very high opinion of himself, was good at everything, and what was left in the world to be achieved, he alone was attempting.

He delighted in telling anyone that would listen, whether animal, vegetable or mineral, that he lived in Cambridge Massachusetts, and lived ten minutes walk from Harvard. He also delighted in telling people that since he moved there twenty years earlier, his IQ had increased by 35 percent.

He was actually born in the wrong country. He should have been born in Nepal, for he was a devout Buddhist, and wore Nepalese clothing underneath his Harris Tweed jacket, with a badge of King Birendra on his lapel. He wore the traditional striped Nepalese prayer cap, and he never went anywhere without it. In the four months he lived next door, I couldn't tell you if he had more hair than a Rastafarian, or if he was as hairless as a boiled egg.

He had a bright red nose, which had a blackhead on the end of it the size of a marrow fat pea. Every time I saw him I wanted to give it a squeeze. But, I feared if I extracted the offending blackhead, his face might cave in. Indeed, if it shot out of his nose, the pressure built up behind it, may sever my head.

He referred to the King of Nepal as His Majesty. He delighted in spouting off about how many times he had been in the Himalayas. Indeed in 1986 – four times in one year.

The reason for such frequent visits to Nepal was due to him having some very influential friends, who were all absolutely minted, as was he, or so he said. They had formed a business consortium to legally cultivate cannabis, as a drug for cancer patients. In most parts of the world, commercial cannabis cultivation was illegal, but not in Nepal at the time.

By day I could hear the tapping of his typewriter, and by night I had the misfortune, along with everyone else on the sixth floor, to be subjected to Mr McKinney's one love. That love was music.

Unfortunately music didn't feel the same way about him. God had not given him the gift of song. In short, his rendition of Cat Stevens' ballad *Morning Has Broken* sounded as if Mr McKinney's voice just had.

One night, Mr McKinney's frequent trips to Nepal were cut short, and he was never to return. It was a very quick decision on his part.

It started with an altercation. Some locals living nearby were fed up of the noise in the middle of the night, and went around to the flat to confront him.

They cornered him on the stairs. To be fair they did wait until he had finished his very bad rendition of *Knocking On Heaven's Door,* and promptly knocked on his.

They dragged him out, protesting and screaming like a two year old. They forced his head through the banisters, twice, and generally gave him a good, old fashioned - public school – Beating, trousers down style.

His calls for assistance to his one and only friend in Nepal, Doctor Singh - a fat bearded Indian who told terrible lies, not least that he was a doctor, a pal of Ranjiv Ghandi, and had graduated from Sandhurst - went predictably unanswered.

Doctor Singh did make a brief appearance on to the landing, to see what all the fuss was about. He made full use of his military training - adopting stealth tactics, by slipping cowardly, but unnoticed into the nearest toilet, locking himself in until the altercation passed.

I, like the doctor, had no intention of helping the man, and watched from the safety of the floor above, as Mr McKinney's head went careering through the banister rails for a third and final time, this time minus his hat.

In the morning, after a brief detour to the police station to file a complaint against the locals, he went to the airport and flew home to increase his IQ further.

I did hear, through a friend, that before the wheels of the aircraft had touched the tarmac, he promptly enrolled himself on a martial arts class for beginners, in a rough ghetto of Boston.

Incidentally - he was bald as a coot!!

Secret Agent 002 Bond – Basildon Bond!!

I've often wondered what it would be like to be Daniel Craig, well not the real Daniel Craig, his character James Bond.

It looks such a glamorous lifestyle being a spy, so adventurous.

Skiing in the Alps in the morning, being chased through the Dolomites by an assassin, base jumping to safety, driving a brand new *Aston Martin* to a secret rendezvous with a gorgeous Russian agent, and then lunch in Venice.

Then in the afternoon, pick up your very own *Sun seeker* power boat, whisk Agent Petrova off to a secluded island, to spend the night dipping your parsnips in the cheese *fondu*, before being flown home in the Prime Ministers very own *learjet*, to be knighted by the queen by the following lunchtime.

This plot could apply to any of the 'Bond' movies. Fleming must have been one of the laziest writer's in history - Sitting on his shaded terrace - in Jamaica, sunbathing, drinking blue mountain coffee by the bucket full, Bob Marley blaring out on his ghetto blaster all day. Laziness only matched by the designers of a famous Stuttgart car manufacturer - every car since 1950 looks the same!

If you want real adventure, I'm your man. Try getting from Bombay to London with twenty quid in your pocket.

I was sitting in the departure lounge at Bombay Airport, waiting for the check-in desk to open, when a Dutch man came and sat by me. We got talking, and he asked me where I was headed. I told him I was flying to Athens. It was my intention to fly back to Greece and start picking fruit, so that I could earn enough money to get back to *'Blighty'*.

I'd actually spent the night in the airport, along with hoards of locals. I 'm not saying I didn't trust them, but, during that particular night, I learned the art of sleeping with one eye open.

It was only when I asked him if he was going to Athens, that I realised the flight landed in Athens, but it then carried on to Amsterdam.

That was where the man was headed.

The cogs started to turn, slowly at first. I realised the plane would land, some people would get off, others would get on, and the rest of the passengers would stay in their seats for half an hour, before taking off again.

Amsterdam is a lot closer to England than Athens, and more importantly, the chance of earning more money, possible factory work, was greater in Holland.

Just one moment I thought. My ticket said Athens, and that is where my bags would be heading.

Then again, what bags? I had a rucksack with a few old clothes and a sleeping bag in it. That was it!!

If I left my sleeping bag in the departure lounge, and took my rucksack on the plane as hand luggage, my rucksack would be with me at all times.

As the check-in opened and I stepped forward, I started to sweat like a Race Horse in a sauna.

The woman behind the desk asked me where I was headed, and I heard myself say: "Athens".

I felt like I was a drug smuggler, but she put her head down, and carried on processing my tickets. She asked me for bags, and I heard myself say: "No – just hand luggage". She looked at my rucksack for what seemed like a minute, but was only a second, then handed me back my passport with my boarding card.

Once I was armed with my boarding card, I was home free. At the departure gate, the stewardess, asked for my passport and boarding pass. Once on board I noted the aircraft was half empty, so I sat in my seat until we took off, then I moved to a different seat. The plane was half empty, because anyone with half a brain would fly KLM to Amsterdam.

As we landed in Athens for a brief stop, my heart almost did. I was as nervous as a kitten. I thought the stewardess would come over to me and say: "Hey aren't you supposed to be getting out here?" but she didn't. She just walked up the aisle and smiled. She asked would I like to move to a less cramped section of the plane. What a result – no one could touch me now.

I was now officially in a different seat to my boarding pass, and if anyone questioned me, i could blame the 'trolley dolly'.

Taking off for Amsterdam, I knew I couldn't be thrown off the plane. It did cross my mind – The joke about the overloaded aircraft. The pilot says to the passengers they will have to lighten the load somehow.

So - the American shouts – "Remember the Alamo", then throws the Mexican out of the plane. I gave a wry smile. It couldn't happen - Could it? Not to me. A burly Mancunian hurls the Scouser out the window. Job done!

As we landed in Schipol, I felt slightly guilty. Of course once in Holland, no one asks to see a boarding pass, and immigration was only interested in my passport. The immigration official was also interested in a pair of foul smelling socks in my rucksack, which I'd forgotten to throw out in Bombay airport.

The sniffer dog made a yelping noise as she found the offending item. However, no one in the building was bothered how I'd arrived in Holland, they were not interested. I'd got a passport, and that was good enough.

Walking out of the airport terminal, minus a pair of stinking old socks, I did feel like James Bond, and relieved. I had thought the unpleasant 'whiff', - detected in the air around seat 35E - was my over active sweat- gland.

It was then I started to think, perhaps I could get all the way to England.

My next obstacle was the train from Amsterdam to Oostende. I still had my twenty pounds, but I may need that for the Channel crossing. My best bet was to board the train, and do my best to avoid the ticket collector. I did extremely well until we got close to the Belgium border. In those days they still had passport control.

Border control usually arrived at the same time as the ticket collector, and that was going to be tricky.

It was then I noticed a carriage of teenage school children. I opened the door to their carriage, and thankfully most Dutch youngsters speak very good English. I explained the situation and asked could I hide under the seat. They loved the idea and agreed to hide me. I was a stowaway. This really was the stuff of James Bond.

They let me crawl under the seat, they sat down and placed bags in the gaps between their feet, blocking me from view.

They were giggling with enthusiasm, but I was very frightened indeed.

I could end up in jail. I heard a man's voice say: "Tickets", then another man say: "Passports". Moments later they were gone. I'd done it.

Before long I found myself at the ferry terminal. I had twenty pound, and an inter rail card that was a year out of date, it might just work I thought.

The cost of a single, four hour crossing to Dover was twenty two pounds. I told the cashier I had an inter rail card which entitled you to half price ferry crossings. I just flashed him the brown wallet, and thankfully, he nodded and asked for eleven pounds.

I'd done it, Bombay to England in less than a day, and still with nine pound to spare.

As we set sail, I sat back in the chair, exhausted. I wasn't exhausted enough not to notice a fine pair of breasts belonging to a statuesque French lady sitting opposite. Her shapely form putting an unnatural strain on her blouse buttons. I closed my eyes, smiled, as thoughts of those cool Himalayan nights came flooding back!!

Acknowledgements

I would like firstly to thank the person who said: *"Everyone has one good book in them"*. I hope you are right. I would also like to thank my dad who told me I was a fool to go travelling, and that if I got stuck, not to think he would bail me out. Thank you Dad, without your words ringing in my ears, I might not have had the adventures that have shaped my life.

Maria Silker who actually said I was funny and should write a book. Some people may agree with you, others will think I'm just odd.

Bec Foulis for doing the initial proof read and correcting my plethora of grammatical errors.

To Lynsey and Andy for turning my project - into something that resembles a book.

To Gary 'Silver Fox' Walker for the sub title.

To Lisa and Susan for listening to me waffle on. Thank you for laughing with me, not at me. That's what friends are for.

To those in work who told me the stories were most amusing, even if the grammar was awful.

Thanks to Mike Madden for his advice on publishing books.

A big thank you to Neil 'Yoda' Kelly – the wise one for thinking up part of the book title.

To Hannah and Siobhan for bringing sunshine in to my life, I hope Hannah grows up to be as adventurous as her tired old dad.

Lastly I'd like to add – The 90s children will grow up flying around the globe, they will have a mobile phone, probably two, in case one breaks. They will take a laptop and have internet access at all times and a couple of credit cards in case they run up a huge 'tab' at a 5 star hotel. They will probably have a web page set up before they go and blog people every day. If not, everyone will know what they are up to every waking minute via *facebook* and *twitter*.

Surely that's not travelling!! Or am I just an old fart.

I sent 3 postcards in 18 months – and one of

them never arrived. But I'm still hopeful.

QUOTATIONS

"... I had ambition not only to go farther than anyone had been before, but as far as it was possible for man to go ..." - James Cook, R.N.

Do just once what others say you can't do, and you will never pay attention to their limitations again." - Captain James Cook.

"The true traveler is he who goes on foot, and even then, he sits down a lot of the time." --Colette, Paris From My Window (1944)

"A man who has the same ideals and prejudices at sixty, as he had at thirty, has wasted thirty years" – Muhammad Ali

"As life is short and the world is vast – the sooner you start to explore the better" – Rouen

"Watch that bow and arrow my lad – You'll have someone's eye out – King Harold of Wessex 1066

"Can someone pass me the toilet paper, and please be quick!!" – Bartholomew Start. 2012

TO BE CONTINPOOED

Hopefully!!

THE AUTHOR

Bartholomew Start - Did not have the best 'start' in life. He was born at the fair ground in Liverpool, to a family of travelling circus folk, who were performing there in 1963.

He was a nervous child, but put that down to the fact his mother was fired out of a cannon whilst pregnant.

Born prematurely and virtually blind, he was forced to wear beer bottle spectacles as a child. Consequently, he didn't mix well.

He was in and out of schools - due to his parent's wanderlust. He started to read about nuclear fusion in his spare time. He told his fellow schoolmates he was off to Cambridge. In 1981, he finally got there - his parent's circus act took them to the outskirts of Huntingdon.

His fascination with pooing began very early. Believe it or not, he started pooing the day he was born. By the age of two he was wiping his own bottom, though not very concisely, and by the age of four he was totally toilet trained and never had another accident until he started travelling at the age of eighteen.

Well apart from a cold snap in 1970, when his mother made him wear long trousers with braces. He got to the toilet, but failed to get them down in time. Not his fault – So does not count.

Bartholomew currently lives in Liverpool with his family, and despite being elderly, continues to poo most days, much to the delight of his daughter, who seems to be a chip off the old block, as she likes nothing better than having a good 'dump', then telling everyone about it.

CAUGHT SHORT ABROAD is his first book.

REVIEWS

This review is from: CAUGHT SHORT ABROAD - My U bend romp around the globe (Kindle Edition)

Funny, ingenuous, gently erudite and intrepid - these are the qualities required by any reader intending to plunge into the bidet of the authors mind. The best travel books can alter the course of your life - this one merely alters the course of your bowels, whilst making you laugh uncontrollably at the most inopportune moment. Forget about Rough guides and Trip advisor, this is the travel companion you need.

This review is from: CAUGHT SHORT ABROAD - My U bend romp around the globe (Kindle Edition)

I'm not a person who can slog through a book, start to finish, so I saved this book for my annul holiday, and I'm glad I did. Come on, we all have to go, and we have all been caught short, it's a fact of life, it happens, live with it. To be able to deliver these unfortunate situations in such an amusing way is a real skill. If you decide to travel the world without the comfort of cash, and five star hotels, this is the result, and very funny too. I was disappointed when I got to the end, I was intrigued how and where his next mishap would happen. A good book to pick up and put down. If you don't laugh at some point, you must be related to the royal family. Check it out.

Amazon Verified Purchase(Who is this?)

This review is from: CAUGHT SHORT ABROAD - My U bend romp around the globe (Kindle Edition)

I laughed so hard during the `Goan Pigs' chapter that I lost all control over my bowels and ended up heavily soiling a beloved pair of tweed trousers and (as a result of rolling off the settee and around on the floor in surprise) my blazer and a significant proportion of the sitting room carpet. Not to mention a small amount of mess on my moustache. I shall be sending Mr Start the cleaning bill. Other than that....BRAVO! A ruddy good read.

Amazon Verified Purchase(<u>What is this?</u>)

This review is from: CAUGHT SHORT ABROAD - My U bend romp around the globe (Kindle Edition)

I really enjoyed reading about Bart's U-Bend adventures around the world! I usually read thrillers or true life crime novels. However, this compilation of short stories is hilarious. I will have to recommend this book to all my family and friends. It is the perfect book to take with you when travelling as the stories are short and keep you entertained throughout.

I can't believe that some of the stories haven't been fabricated ! ! ! However, true or not the stories are well written and very amusing. The author is certainly a very funny guy and I look forward to his next publication.

Amazon Verified Purchase(<u>What is this?</u>)

This review is from: CAUGHT SHORT ABROAD - My U bend romp around the globe (Kindle Edition)

Downloaded this book as it was a Kindle freebie. Thought I could read it when I ran out of other books to read (as if that is possible with a Kindle). Needing a change of pace from other genre, I decided to give this book a "go". Can't recall when I have laughed so long and loud. I laughed so hard that the tears were running down my leg. At one point I had to make a mad dash to the loo. Thankfully no one was blocking my way or demanding an entrance fee and I had an unlimited supply of toilet rolls. If you enjoy toilet humour, then give this book a go. Having read it now, I would gladly have paid for it. Am in the process of emailing my Kindle friends to recommend.

Amazon Verified Purchase(What is this?)

This review is from: CAUGHT SHORT ABROAD - My U bend romp around the globe (Kindle Edition)

A very high turd per page ratio. Bartholomew Start makes Tom Sharpe books look like reference manuals.
This is gonzo Literature at it's best. It will appeal to every blokes love affair with the toilet.
If this book was 'improved' grammatically ,by the pen of a 'serious' copy writer it would not be the hilarious romp it is. Don't change a thing. Not everyone wants to
read Wordsworth - Sometimes you just need a good laugh.

Mankind needs a follow up Mr Start. Go travelling an recant your tales of woe.

Where have you been all my life. This book is absolutely Bumstatic.

Amazon Verified Purchase(What is this?)

This review is from: CAUGHT SHORT ABROAD - My U bend romp around the globe (Kindle Edition)

Read the book in a few hours... still chuckling as I write this. Very, very funny. Advisable not to read it in public as onlookers will be calling for the men in white coats!
It is rare that a book is produced in which virtually every paragraph will have you laughing out loud.
Laughter is definitely the best medicine, and you will be feeling much better having read this book.
Whether you will want to broaden your horizons by following in Mr Start's footsteps is another matter entirely!

This review is from: CAUGHT SHORT ABROAD - My U bend romp around the globe (Kindle Edition)

If you enjoy toilet humour, this is the book for you! I loved it. It's a wickedly funny journey of potty based humour around the globe. Anyone who has travelled to less developed countries will empathise with the author, I certainly do. A great book to dip in and out of, each chapter is short and can be read non-sequentially. Some of the incidents were laugh out loud hilarious.

Amazon Verified Purchase(What is this?)

This review is from: CAUGHT SHORT ABROAD - My U bend romp around the globe (Kindle Edition)

Not so much a book, more a series of hilarious buttock clenching anecdotes.
Highlights include explaining a strange geographical feature after a cycle ride ,
a job interview never to forget,an awkward meeting with partner's parents, a snuffling pig.
I haven't laughed so much and simultaneously clenched ever! The tales are realistically graphic.
A unique take on a travel 'log', Just on the crude side of vulgar and very funny.
Read it but make sure you are near some reliable porcelain.

Amazon Verified Purchase(What is this?)

This review is from: CAUGHT SHORT ABROAD - My U bend romp around the globe (Kindle Edition)

From the pen of Merseysides fastest growing writing sensation comes a rip-roaring, split your sides, and never laughed so much in my life masterpiece. Sit back, relax and join Bartholomew Start on his buttock clenching journey around the globe. If there's only one book that you plan to buy this year then make sure it's Caught Short Abroad.

2914524R00089

Printed in Great Britain
by Amazon.co.uk, Ltd.,
Marston Gate.